For Johnnie -
May the stories
in this collection inspire
you - Fondly!
Marcia

Join
your
Newcomer
Wishes,
Dave Smits

RECOLLECTIONS OF OUR PEACE CORPS SERVICE 1963-1965

Kick-Off, Life in Guatemala, and Afterwards

PEACE
CORPS
WRITERS

COMPILED BY RAMONA WHALEY
EDITED BY DAVE SMITS

TO order Book:
  CreateSpace.com/3743137
        or
  Amazon.com

ISBN: 193592513X
ISBN 13: 9781935925132
Library of Congress Control Number: 2012938158

TABLE OF CONTENTS

SECTION I

Roads To The Peace Corps And The Training Experience

Johnnie – I am glad you enjoyed learning about Guatemala, Charlie Carreras

Thank you for sharing a wonderful time during our lives

Pat Smits

SECTION II

Service In Guatemala

SECTION III

Thereafter

APPENDICES

Let there be peace!
Evelyn Glasscock

RECOLLECTIONS OF OUR PEACE CORPS SERVICE 1963-1965

Kick-Off, Life in Guatemala, and Afterwards

PEACE CORPS WRITERS

COMPILED BY RAMONA WHALEY
EDITED BY DAVE SMITS

ACKNOWLEDGMENT

We in Guatemala III would like to acknowledge our profound indebtedness to Ramona Whaley, without whose inspirational and tireless efforts these Recollections would never have seen the light of day. It was Ramona who conceptualized them, motivated us to make contributions, and had the patience and perseverance to organize them in presentable form. Thanks Ramona.

INTRODUCTION

The timing was surreal. The consequences were life-changing.

A half-century ago, a generation of Americans, mostly in their early twenties, was on the cusp of major life decisions: "What on earth do I really want to do now?"

Motivations were many and varied, but at least 69 trainees for Guatemala were affected by the unconventional challenge cast out by a newly elected, charismatic young president: "Will you go to Ghana for two years to help improve the health conditions in that country? Will you dedicate two years of your life to education in Latin America?"

Sue Hetzel, Pat Smits, and Tim Kraft had heard Kennedy speak on their college campuses in Wisconsin and New Hampshire in 1960, and from that time on were hopefully fixated on the creation of this vague "Corps for Peace."

Later generations would apply for the Peace Corps after being persuaded by a far-flung college recruiting program. They would miss, however, the inimitable Boston-accented call to be the test flight of a new idea and a controversial program.

Guatemala III would also share the "black anguish," as Carole Oliver wrote, of being with the group at lunch and incredulously hearing the news on Nov. 22, 1963. "How we continued on in training through December," she wondered, "I just do not recall, but I do know that I wanted more than ever to go to Guatemala."

Collectively, our group was a mixed bag, including representatives of the African-American, Hispanic-American, Japanese-Chamorro, and Jewish cultural traditions.

There was a grandmother of nine who spent her 65th birthday scaling peaks and rappelling cliffs in nearby mountains as part of our physical and psychological testing. There were eight married couples, including one couple in their 50s with children, and one engaged pair.

We were committed, energetic, good-humored and, for all our different backgrounds, a remarkably congenial group. Not everyone stayed with the program; some left for whatever personal misgivings; others were, in the bureaucratic jargon of the day, "selected out" by program directors. Fifty-eight of us continued to Guatemala.

When we signed up, we had NO idea what our training would entail. In hindsight, it was well-organized given its newness, but in other respects, wildly irrelevant. For example, we spent two class days learning how and why not to try to build a dam.

While our program did inform us that we would be at work under a country's military dictatorship, we didn't learn a whole lot about the CIA-directed coup in 1954 that would install this kind of regime. Tragically, the change lead to over 80,000 deaths from the time of our service to the late '80s.

Were we naive in many respects? Of course. But we went. We learned. We worked. We returned and stayed involved . . . and, perhaps more than most groups, we kept in touch.

Were we an extraordinary or select group? We have no way of comparing ourselves to others, and what would be the point? But if re-entry service is any kind of barometer, please read the homecoming section of this book. If reunions are a sign of camaraderie, Guatemala III has traveled to Virginia, Washington, New Jersey, California and Guatemala to meet in sizable numbers. Mini-reunions, too numerous to mention have occurred in several states and several Central American countries. We are a close group.

Before Ramona Whaley cracked a whip to urge us to write, who knew that so many of our group could recall their motives, fears and reservations, their life and death experiences, the grand adventure and ongoing friendships of Guatemala III and Guatemala? All of it is told in a very articulate and moving way. Take your time. Read every page.

Tim Kraft

SECTION I

ROADS TO THE PEACE CORPS AND THE TRAINING EXPERIENCE

IN THE SPRING OF '63

By Bernie Engel

My decision to apply to the Peace Corps was made, quite frankly, on a lark. It was 1963. It was in the spring of my senior year at Miami University (Ohio).

I had been accepted into the law school at Washington University in St. Louis. I had been programmed to do this, not necessarily Washington U., but law school.

As the second son of Eastern European Jewish immigrants, I was destined for a legal career. My older brother had already done four years at Harvard, on full scholarship, and was then in his last year of medical school. My older sister had married after her first year of college — also part of "the program." I mean, why else send a daughter to college?

So, with a doctor in the family and the likelihood of grandchildren in the near future, it remained only for me to head off to law school to complete the program and allow my parents to hold up their heads in the community and walk proudly to the synagogue in the knowledge that they had fulfilled a small part of God's plan for them and the Jewish people.

Don't ask me why I walked into the Peace Corps recruiting office that spring day. I really wish I could say it was a well-thought-out decision based on political, social or humanitarian considerations.

But, it wasn't. It was just something to do.

Let's be frank here. I was, at the age of twenty-two, a really immature college senior. It was a lark, something different, something to talk to my fraternity brothers about. "Hey, guess what I did today. I went to the Peace Corps office! Ain't that cool."

Inertia, however, can be a wonderful thing. I took the papers. Filled them out. Sent them in. Never really thinking about what I was doing. Inertia.

Much to my surprise, the Peace Corps said "OK. You're going to Guatemala."

Wait a minute. Now what?

I think at that point I made one of my more rational decisions and that was to write to Washington University and tell them thanks for the spot at the law school, but I'd have to pass. They were kind enough to write back and say they'd hold a place for me if I still wanted it two years down the road.

That, of course, left my parents.

Timing, except on stage, has never been my strong suit. Had I half a brain, I would have waited until after graduation to tell my parents, my father in particular — that God's plan was going to be interrupted and that I was planning (in my dad's view) to bring eternal shame on the family.

But, no.

The morning of my graduation, my parents and (thank God) my brother were at my apartment for breakfast prior to heading off to the stadium for the commencement ceremony.

"Uh, Dad — about law school. Well, there's this program called the Peace Corps and I've decided to join up."

No reaction.

"Is this something connected to the law school?"

"Uh, no, Dad — it's a government thing."

"Oh, it's something you'll be doing over the summer? They'll pay you?"

"Uh, no, Dad — it's something that's outside the country and it's for two years. I won't be going to law school this fall."

Silence.

At that, he asked me if I was crazy. I won't repeat some of the other things he said. Suffice it to say that he grabbed my mother and walked out of the apartment, fully intending to get in the car and drive back to Cleveland.

My brother ran out to stop him. My father was prone to listen to my brother since he was a doctor (well, almost a doctor) and doctors occupy a hallowed, almost mystical position in our community. My brother convinced my father to stay for the graduation, promising that we would talk about this Peace Corps business on our return to Cleveland.

It took much of the summer, but we finally came to a truce based on my promise to reconsider law school when I was done with "this Guatewhatcha cowboy business."

WHY PEACE CORPS?

By Charlie Carreras

I first heard of the Peace Corps when it was mentioned in the 1960 Presidential election campaign. I concluded right away that I was going to join it. I knew I wanted eventually to get a Ph. D. and to teach, but I signed up for two years in the Peace Corps first, soon after it was created on March 1, 1961. In September of 1963, I began training in Las Cruces, NM.

Why Peace Corps?

I went into the Peace Corps because I was motivated by John F. Kennedy's New Frontier agenda. And, yes, Kennedy's inaugural speech, delivered as only JFK could, had a lot to do with it: "Ask not what your country can do for you — ask what you can do for your country."

I had read a book, The Ugly American, a couple years earlier. It was about the United States' foreign aid programs that did not do what they were supposed to do.

But now our country was going to be different, and we volunteers were going to help make that difference. The Peace Corps was going to allow us to live out our ideals.

I was really excited about going to Latin America. I wanted to learn all I could about my assigned country. I had fallen in love with Mexican history as an undergraduate and I knew I wanted to go there or to Central America *and to do something!* When I got my assignment to live and work in Guatemala, it was perfect.

After reading The Ugly American, I had concluded that I could do my small part to improve our relations with Latin America.

I *had* to do it!

A COLLEGE-INSPIRED PEACE CORPS DECISION

By Dave Snyder

My wife, Sally, grew up primarily in Ohio, while I lived in various parts of the country: Massachusetts, Illinois, Connecticut, Ohio, and even Hawaii.

We met in 1959. It was the summer after our senior year in high school in Hudson, Ohio. We dated from then until we married in April, 1963, the same year Sally graduated from Lesley College in Cambridge, MA, and I, from Wesleyan University.

It was my idea to join the Peace Corps. My years at Wesleyan were a major influence since the school was always liberal and "into" causes.

Many of my classmates were involved in freedom marches in the South. Martin Luther King, Jr. spoke at Wesleyan twice while I was there. One of my roommates spent the summer of his junior year in Africa with Operation Crossroads.

Sally and I applied to, and were accepted into, three programs: International Voluntary Services for rural community development in Vietnam; Acción, for community development in Caracas; and the Peace Corps, for community development in Guatemala.

I was very interested in IVS-Vietnam, but got a lot of flack from Sally's parents about our safety. A Wesleyan classmate who chose Vietnam was ambushed and killed there two years later, so I guess my in-laws were right. After doing a little research, we chose PC-Guatemala over Acción-Venezuela. Frankly, neither of us knew much about Latin America.

When our Peace Corps training was delayed by dengue fever in Puerto Rico, we decided to see some of the western United States and Canada. We took machine shop jobs for six weeks in Ft. Morgan, CO, saved money, and continued traveling, even camping roadside in our tent because the parks were too expensive. We traveled for six weeks, then returned home to Ohio with a quarter tank of gas and our last five dollars.

We were ready for the Peace Corps.

JFK, GRANDMOTHER AND THE MISSIONARY

By Lynda Sanderford Morrison

President John F. Kennedy's words inspired me to join the Peace Corps — a chance to serve in a meaningful way — but there were other influences as well. One was my grandmother, who could always hold my rapt attention with her stories, until the funny parts, when she began to giggle and could never finish. She had a missionary friend in India who returned to the States periodically to raise money with a slide show at the church. My grandmother passed her friend's accounts of her life in India on to me. (It is interesting how some of us in Guatemala were influenced so much by missionaries.)

I had a fascination with anything and anyone from another culture and a soft spot for immigrants.

When I went off to the University of North Carolina at Chapel Hill in my junior year, I was paired with a foreign student at my request and we became best friends for life. She was a Cuban who had just escaped the Castro regime by coming to the U.S. as a student. Her troubles became part of my family's devotion as we tried to get her younger brother out of Cuba before he stumbled into real trouble. Her mother and father eventually followed.

When my first invitation for Peace Corps service in Malaysia came, I turned it down because I knew I wanted to learn Spanish and more about Latin America. Leaving for training with Guatemala III at New Mexico State University in Las Cruces was the beginning of a great adventure for me. As the plane landed at a stop in Midland, Texas, it kicked up a lot of swirling dust clouds. Through them, I could see a genuine cowboy leaning against a post near the gate. I knew for certain I was out West and on my own.

What I remember most from training was the mountain climbing and how the rain started before I made it to the top. Water was rushing over the rock wall and washing mosses from crevices into my eyes.

I kept thinking, "If I don't do this, will I be washed out of the program, literally?"

Finally, I heard someone say, "Only a fly can go up a glass wall," and they lowered us not too gently to the ground.

I KNEW WE WERE INVINCIBLE!

By Bob Hetzel

As I traveled to Las Cruces, NM, for Peace Corps training in the fall of 1963, I felt buoyed with optimism about making the world a better place!

My belief that being an American with a college degree and a desire to serve would be sufficient to be of some value was, of course, naïve and a little arrogant.

There was also the thrill of anticipated adventure in a foreign land, Las Cruces, for a start. Even going that far from home was exciting and a little frightening. I thought New Mexico was the developing world.

Living on a college campus at New Mexico State University, however, made me feel right at home, from eating in the school cafeteria to staying in the dorms that housed Guatemala III volunteers during our three months of training.

Most of all, there was that youthful optimism free of any doubt that the world could be a better place and that we could make it happen.

It was a confidence and optimism that grew throughout the training period and was strengthened by meeting fellow volunteers. It sealed the deal meeting Keni Kent and Tony Durán, the CARE director and assistant director in Guatemala, who did double duty as directors for the Guatemala III Peace Corps volunteers.

I *knew* we were *invincible*.

PROUD TO BE A "KENNEDY KID"

By Carole Oliver

I wonder sometimes how a young woman from Monrovia, CA, could have believed back in the 1960s that she could make a difference in the world. I, like so many of us, had been swept up by John F. Kennedy's challenging words, "Ask not what your country can do for you — ask what you can do for your country!"

Here was a young man elected to the presidency, full of courage and eloquence, speaking of peace and justice, and freedom from hunger and disease for all mankind. He called for each of us, including me, to try to make that happen.

My father and mother had instilled in me the values of justice and equality, of duty and responsibility, not just the rights of being an American citizen. I was a junior in college when President Kennedy announced the establishment of the Peace Corps in March of 1961. I knew immediately that I wanted to join, if my country would have me. I said goodbye to my mother (my dad, whom I adored, was a U.S. history teacher who died in the same year JFK was elected president) and arrived in Las Cruces, NM, for Peace Corps training at New Mexico State University in September, 1963.

If all went well, I would be going to Guatemala. Somehow, this training was to turn me into a Spanish-speaking, rural community-development worker who would be well versed in Guatemalan history and culture.

I wanted to bring hope into the world. Was I idealistic? Naïve? I would have answered no at the time, but the truth is, I knew so little. I had so much to learn.

I was among those known as "Kennedy's Kids," or "Kennedy's Kiddie Corps" — not exactly a compliment at the time, but I am so proud of that now!

A few weeks later (even now my tears well up thinking of it), my president was dead. My hero had been struck down.

That early morning of Nov. 22, 1963, had been full of life and an innocence so quickly gone. Color turned to gray, and then to black anguish — dull, uncertain, incomprehensible.

A new, dangerous world stared back at us as we watched in shock the televised news of President John F. Kennedy's assassination. We tried to comprehend it all.

How we continued training through December, I do not recall, but I do know I wanted more than ever to go to Guatemala.

I wanted to prove to those cynical pessimists in the Congress and in the press that we were not just naïve, idealistic kids (which we were), and mostly I wanted to prove that our president had been right.

I wanted to prove that the Peace Corps could make a difference in the world.

I HEARD KENNEDY SPEAK ELOQUENTLY

By Sue Pitt

On the balmy afternoon of March 24, 1960, during my freshman year at the University of Wisconsin-Madison, I strolled alone along the shore of Lake

Mendota to the music hall to hear a speaker then little known to me.

John F. Kennedy had been campaigning in the presidential primary since January, spending a lot of time in Wisconsin and Minnesota. What other time might I have the opportunity to hear in a fairly intimate setting of several hundred people a potential future president of the United States?

Seated in the back of the crowded hall, I could feel the flurry of activity of Kennedy's six or seven personal organizers. The men in dark suits exuded importance. Yet Kennedy stood out among his contingent.

The experience for me was magical. It wasn't only his flair, the dark suit and wide pin tie, but his carefully groomed dark hair and, at 42 years old, his youthful good looks.

Then he spoke — so eloquently.

He spoke of the wealth of our country spent on the arms race with the Soviet Union and the threat of a nuclear war. He explained Russia's capability of firing missiles at the United States. He said America could not stand aside while the enemies of freedom extended communist control over the whole southern half of the globe.

Just a few years before, Kennedy had become a member of the Senate Committee on Foreign Relations. There his emphasis turned from military programs to economic aid to underdeveloped countries, his double-edged sword for defeating communism and spreading freedom.

I began viewing Kennedy as a Servant Leader, someone who would foster the advancement of people throughout the world to attain world peace. How could peace be achieved if the majority of the world's population was living in poverty? In his University of Wisconsin speech, Kennedy asked Americans to "share in the great common task of bringing to man that decent way of life that is the foundation of freedom and a condition of peace."

Later, as volunteers in Guatemala, we discussed over and over the question of what those basic needs were: Education? Jobs? Health? People in the communities where we worked would often decide. For example, when we wanted to bring in *planchas* [metal sheets] for latrines, everyone signed up. But then they said, "What we *really* need is a new school for our children and teacher, since the tile roof is leaking and the walls are caving in and there are no windows."

Although the Kennedy Library categorizes his University of Wisconsin talk as an armament speech, it was the reason I joined the Peace Corps.

On April 5, 1960, twelve days after I heard Kennedy's speech, he won the Wisconsin primary. That November he was elected president, and four months later, on March 1, 1961, he created the Peace Corps.

Kennedy's speech further impacted me because I had just gone on spring break in the Deep South with high school friends. There, I witnessed segregation firsthand.

My friends Izzy, Aileen, Judy and I hit the Ft. Lauderdale beach scene via Greyhound, not too proud or particular to take turns trying to sleep on the aisle floor in the back of the bus. When we stopped and got out of the bus, we were shocked and disgusted to see the "Whites Only" signs in the bathrooms and at the "bubblers" (water fountains). Those shabby bathrooms symbolized for me the injustice of racism in the United States. Racism was a sad reality of life in the early '60s.

In the spring of 1962, the Cuban Missile Crisis stopped us all in our tracks. There was palpable fear that life as we knew it was ending. A communist leader was threatening us in our own backyard.

Kennedy's "armament speech" was substantiated and his eloquent invitation to participate in a Corps for Peace was much too important and beautiful to decline. We eagerly filled out the applications.

A "DIFFERENT ROAD" LED TO PEACE CORPS

By Ramona Whaley

"Two roads diverged...and I – I took the one...that has made all the difference."
— Robert Frost

Detouring from my routine route to class at Georgetown College one day near the end of my senior year led me to the Peace Corps and Guatemala. Whether the detour was divine guidance, fickle fate or meaningless meandering is debatable, but it took me to a campus building where Peace Corps recruiters sat at a long table piled high with pamphlets. And that has made all the difference!

"For Carol!" my mind immediately shouted. "Carol's the missionary type! She'll do this!" Grabbing an armload of brochures, I hurried to my dorm and dumped the ton of Peace Corps literature on my unimpressed roommate's desk. The brochures urged youths to devote two years out of their lives, to put professional careers on hold, and to volunteer helping strangers in remote Third World villages. Thanks, but no thanks, said Carol, who headed directly into teaching as planned.

As for me, I was eager to finish college, get out in the real world, and set it on fire with journalistic brilliance. That agenda got sidetracked because I glanced too long at the Peace Corps information while trashing it. I read it and got hooked.

I wish I could say that altruism motivated me to join the Peace Corps, but that is not so. The lure of adventure, romanticized in the memorable music of the '60s, called to me, especially "Far Away Places" and Gogi Grant's "The Wayward Wind." Except for a 1962 spring break trip to Florida, I had hardly even crossed the Kentucky state line. I wanted to know what was beyond my pleasantly rural home town of Fern Creek. The Peace Corps was a travel opportunity, albeit no frills, and that was mostly why I signed up.

As it turned out, the Peace Corps was so much more than the travel I craved! Most significantly, I got an education about, and a deep affection for, the people of my host country. I burned to come home and tell my own countrymen about all those wonderful, unforgettable villagers we in Guatemala III lived and worked with, teaching them more efficient ways of living.

The most relevant and lasting legacy of my Peace Corps service was the very changed person I became and the different ways I came to view the world and all our planet's peoples.

Was my campus detour a mere chance? Or did it make "all the difference," as the poet Robert Frost wrote. You decide.

OFF TO A NEW ADVENTURE

By Jay Jackson

In 1940, the year I was born, the United States was still recovering from the Great Depression. In just over a year, the country would be in all-out war with Japan in the Pacific and the Axis powers in Europe.

My dad wanted to be part of the war effort. Everyone in the tiny close-knit community called Highgrove, situated in the orange groves between Riverside and Colton, CA, knew my father and his family. Prior to my parents' marriage, my mom had been secretary to the gossip columnist Jimmy Fiddler in Hollywood. The son of a Baptist minister, Bob Jackson (my dad) was the local postmaster, clerk in the community's only grocery store, and editor of Highgrove's monthly newspaper. He printed a special edition announcing my birth on Oct. 25, 1940.

In his mid-thirties, my dad was too old to enlist in military service. He signed up instead with the American Red Cross to support U.S. troops in the Pacific. The decision would take him during the next six years to the Philippines, far from his family and home.

At war's end, Dad was offered a position with the American Red Cross in the Philippines, and had the option to bring his family along. Mom, my older sister Judy and I were all packed and ready to go!

Mom's family thought our moving to the Philippines was a wild idea. We would be too far away from Dad — so far that we could only talk to him by ham radio at strange hours of the day and night. And, it would be far too dangerous, with an on-going insurgency movement called the Huk Rebellion being fought there.

Mom's parents talked her out of moving. I felt deprived of a wonderful adventure, which probably contributed to my life-long passion for foreign travel.

Dad returned to the States as assistant director of the Red Cross unit at March Field Air Force Base outside Riverside, CA, when I was in the second grade. Three years later, he was offered the position of assistant manager with the Portland, OR, Red Cross. Dad prepared us for the move by taking us on a trip to Oregon the summer preceding the move. It was my first trip outside southern California, except for a trip or two into Tijuana, Mexico.

In Portland, I got a paper route, delivering the Portland Oregonian, the daily morning newspaper. By selling enough subscriptions to the paper for the Rose Parade edition in the summer of 1953, I won a trip with other news carriers to Victoria, British Columbia. That trip, by bus and overnight ferry, was the first time I traveled outside the United States on my own.

In 1954, our family moved again, to Eugene, OR, where my dad became chapter manager for the Lane County Red Cross and I started eighth grade at Roosevelt Junior High. Our family, though not poor, was by no means wealthy, and dad, concerned about the Red Cross's tight budget, would frequently turn down salary raises, despite our family's own needs.

To help out, I got another paper route, mowed lawns and babysat to earn pocket money, buy clothes, and save for college, which I knew my parents couldn't afford. I always assumed I would attend college, in part because of living in a college town.

When I got to college, the University of Oregon, I was less interested in academics than student activities. I became president of the campus YMCA my freshman year, and chairman of the World University Service committee my sophomore year. The spring fundraiser I organized was WUS's most successful U.S. event that year, raising more than $5,000.

The success was due in part to a shack we built on campus to symbolize how some students live in other parts of the world. My Sig Ep fraternity constructed the tiny shack out of cardboard and other scraps assembled overnight at the main campus intersection in front of the student union.

The project resulted in front-page photos in the Daily Emerald, the university newspaper. In letters to the editor, some called for its removal, while others lauded the effort to draw student attention to a cause outside their daily lives. As a result, World University Service got great publicity for its week-long activities.

At the end of my junior year, I was selected to chaperone a bus of high school students traveling cross-country under the American Field Service foreign-student exchange program. My group included 54 students who had lived in, and attended high school in, Oregon during the previous school year.

Over 2,000 students and their chaperones gathered at the University of Massachusetts at Amherst. We traveled on to New York City and then Washington, D.C., where we met President John F. Kennedy in the White House Rose Garden during the early days of "Camelot."

Seeing the United States, visiting the White House and living for three weeks with foreign students was a watershed experience for me. I wanted to see the world!

I learned during my senior year that World University Service was organizing an Asian studies seminar.

Participants would spend three months in Asia, studying the cultures of Japan, Hong Kong, Thailand, Burma, India and Pakistan. I applied and was accepted, the youngest of 29 participants, including several university professors, a Catholic priest, two YWCA directors and two college presidents.

There was one hitch. In exchange for this round-the-world opportunity, I would be required to work for World University Service as a campus organizer for the 1962-1963 school year.

That summer seminar again exposed me to different cultures and kindled my desire to do something undefined but meaningful in the world.

At summer's end, I returned to the United States for a week's orientation in New York City to become the World University Service field representative for the western United States. The job entailed traveling primarily by bus and train to more than 100 college campuses in the sprawling region stretching from Dallas (my base), north to Indianapolis and west to Seattle.

When I returned to the University of Oregon in April, 1963, to complete my studies, I found that all eligible young men were being called up for the Vietnam War draft. I did not want to go to war, so I applied for the Peace Corps just before graduating that year.

The Peace Corps would give me an opportunity to think about my future and to respond to JFK's inaugural challenge: "Ask not what your country can do for you — ask what you can do for your country."

When I applied to the Peace Corps, I thought I would be going to Africa. When my invitation for Guatemala came, I had to consult the atlas to see where it was located. To my surprise, it was in Central America.

When news arrived that my training group would meet in New York City to travel together to Puerto Rico for an Outward Bound training and bonding experience, I was very excited.

I decided to leave Eugene a few days before the whole group was to meet in New York. Consequently, I missed the telegram from Peace Corps Washington stating that the scheduled Puerto Rico training had been cancelled.

In New York, after a few days of touring, I went to the appointed gathering place, as instructed by the Peace Corps, only to find that our Puerto Rico training had been cancelled due to an outbreak of dengue fever on the island. The few of us who got to New York as originally scheduled were told to go home and await further instruction. We were each given a month's per diem and an airplane ticket back home.

With the Peace Corps per diem burning holes in our pockets, Bryce Hamilton — another trainee I had just met — and I decided to have some fun in New York before going home. We went to the United Nations, climbed the Pan Am building, which was still under construction, and visited Greenwich Village and various other sites in the city.

I found out there was a civil rights march being organized in Washington, D.C. and free bus travel was being offered. I joined 100,000 others participating in the "March on Washington," where Martin Luther King, Jr. made his famous "I Have A Dream" speech. It was an electrifying moment and I felt that I was a part of history.

When I returned to Eugene, word arrived that I was to report to New Mexico State University at Las

Cruces. At the ripe old age of 23, I was one of the older trainees. Most in the group were 21 or 22, having just graduated from college.

My family saw me off at the airport and I flew off to a new adventure!

ON THE ROAD TO LAS CRUCES

By Susan Stapleton McAvey

If I had a hammer, I'd hammer out justice,
I'd ring the bell of freedom,
And I'd sing about the love between my brothers and my sisters,
All over this land.
(Seeger/Hayes) From the album PETER,
 PAUL and MARY.

As we drove into our nation's capital the morning of Aug. 28, 1963, the city looked like a ghost town. Few people were on the streets — no cars, no buses — but we saw barricades in front of government buildings and military personnel guarding them. They were preparing for rioting and vandalism because 250,000 people were about to arrive from all over the country.

I stood on the National Mall and looked around me. In every direction, I saw people of every age, every ethnic group, young and old, short and tall.

The statue of President Lincoln, the great emancipator, gazed over humanity from his landmark memorial and seemed to approve of what was taking place.

Soon Dr. Martin Luther King, Jr. began to speak from the steps of the memorial. To this day, when I hear Dr. King's words, I experience the same feelings I had on that long-ago day, especially when I hear his concluding words: "When we let freedom ring, when we let it ring from every village and every hamlet, from every state and every city, we will be able to speed up that day when all of God's children, black men and white men, Jews and Gentiles, Protestants and Catholics, will be able to join hands and sing in the words of the old Negro spiritual, 'Free at last! Free at last! Thank God almighty, we are free at last.'"

I feel certain that President John Kennedy was scrutinizing those events from the White House. He is the reason I was there that day. My unexpected privilege of participating in the March on Washington for civil rights for all Americans was my first stop on the way to becoming part of JFK's "New Frontier" as a Peace Corps volunteer.

I was supposed to be in Puerto Rico that day, training with the third group of volunteers assigned to serve in Guatemala, Central America. But, there was a dengue fever epidemic in Puerto Rico, and we would train instead at New Mexico State University in Las Cruces, NM, but not until late September.

I had spent the summers of 1962 and 1963 working as a counselor at a girls' camp in Maryland. The camp had originally been only for white children. In 1962 it was integrated for the first time. I recall what happened when we took those seven- and eight-year-old campers to an amusement park and pool on the Chesapeake Bay. After several hours, the manager approached and told us we had to leave because we had brought a child of color. Our return transportation would not arrive for several hours, so he said we could stay, but the child had to be kept in a confined area, and to make her less conspicuous, she had to wear her swim cap all the time. We told the girls they all had to wear their swim caps, so they wouldn't lose them. None objected.

Earlier that summer, the Peace Corps had informed me that I was to report to New York City on Aug. 25 and from there we would leave for training in Puerto Rico. They failed to reach me with a message about the cancelled training. When I arrived at our rendez-vous point in New York City, I was the last of four volunteers they had not reached in advance about the changed plans.

My camp's staff had accompanied me to New York to see me off on my exciting foreign adventure. I returned to Washington, D. C. and spent a few days with the staff. That placed me in the city on the day of the March on Washington. The camp director's office was a short walk to the National Mall.

That day, I was privileged to hear one of the world's greatest orators deliver an address known throughout the world. And, they say, he didn't even have notes!

There was another sound that day on the mall — Bob Dylan, from my own home state of Minnesota, sang "The times they are a changin'." Joan Baez and Peter, Paul and Mary protested in song the pain of poverty and social injustice, as they pleaded for peace and love rather than a world of war and tyranny. In their poetic words, they too, were responding to President Kennedy's challenge, "Ask not what your country can do for you —- ask what you can do for your country."

One of the wonders of that day occurred as the program ended and the people walked back to the thousands of buses waiting to take them to their homes all over this land. There was no rioting, no vandalism and no buildings were damaged.

That unexpected stop on my way to the Peace Corps made such an impact on me that, year after year, I educated countless classes of fascinated students about the day in August, 1963, when I and 250,000 unified strangers marched on Washington to promote justice, equality and civil rights for all Americans.

THE STATE OF THE WORLD AND
MY LIFE PRIOR TO THE PEACE CORPS

By Dave Smits

I grew up in the Fox River Valley in northeastern Wisconsin just south of Green Bay. The fate of most of my male high school classmates was to go to work in one of the local paper mills, which brought employment and prosperity, along with air and water pollution reminiscent of the environmental devastation widespread in late nineteenth-century America.

As a boy, I loved to fish, but there were neither fish nor any other living thing in the Fox River. It was utterly defiled by the discharged wastes from the mills. On hot and humid August days, the mills spewed the overpowering smell of sulfur dioxide, a rotten-egg odor that took our breath away and permeated the clothes we wore. Local residents didn't complain about environmental desecration; they accepted it as the price to be paid for good jobs.

I was determined not to work in any of the paper mills. After graduation, I planned to see the world and never return to my suffocating hometown. My parents were simple people who had no interest in travel and I had visited only one other state besides Wisconsin, namely upper Michigan.

I joined a U.S. Naval Reserve unit in Green Bay while still in high school, and went on two-week annual summer cruises to learn seafaring. I also signed up for two years of active duty in the regular Navy.

In 1956, after graduating from high school, I headed for the Great Lakes Naval Training Center in northern Illinois. The anti-war hysteria associated with Vietnam had not yet raised its head and I viewed World War II veterans as role models. The subsequent Korean War was a frustrating and bloodstained struggle that ended in a stalemate, but the GIs who returned from Korea were not vilified. Military service, from my perspective, was an honorable obligation and my chance to let the badger out.

In boot camp at Great Lakes, my company had a five-foot-six-inch drill instructor who had no liking for big men or human failings. I learned quickly to shut my mouth and obey orders.

After boot camp, I was assigned to the USS Boston (CAG-1), our nation's first guided missile cruiser, and a bonafide showboat. The U.S. Navy sent it far and wide to impress our communist adversaries. I had joined the Navy to see the world and I soon saw a lot of it from the main deck of the Boston. I'm a "shellback," which means I have crossed the equator, and a "blue nose," because I have crossed the Arctic Circle. I went through the Panama Canal, sailed in the Mediterranean and Caribbean, and in 1958, visited Cuba.

I was by then a third-class petty officer, assigned shore patrol duty for sailors on liberty in "Gitmo City," Cuba's leading den of vice for sailors and marines.

Armed only with nightsticks, shore patrolmen were to preserve order among the drunken "swabbies" who descended in hordes on the bars and brothels just outside the U.S. naval base at Guantanamo Bay.

The tensions in the place were heightened by the presence everywhere of heavily armed "Batistianos." They were the thugs and enforcers who kept in power the island's dictator, Fulgencio Batista, our puppet in Cuba. Those enforcers made available to our sailors commercialized vice of staggering proportions. Among their other pastimes, they pimped for the prostitutes who abounded on the island. An estimated 11,500 prostitutes earned their living in Havana alone in the year I was in Cuba. Arthur Schlesinger, Jr., President Kennedy's special assistant, recalled a visit to Havana in the 1950s:

> I was enchanted by Havana, and appalled by the way that lovely city was being debased into a great casino and brothel for American businessmen over for a big weekend from Miami. My fellow countrymen reeled through the streets, picking up fourteen-year-old Cuban girls and tossing coins to make men scramble in the gutter. One wondered how any Cuban — on the basis of this evidence — could regard the United States with anything but hatred.[1]

It was also evident that the Batistianos I encountered were edgy and agitated. By the summer of 1958 it was becoming clear that the Batista regime was doomed. Fidel Castro's guerillas in the Sierra Maestra (among them, allegedly, a former high-school

---

1   Quoted in Louis A. Perez, Jr., Cuba: Between Reform and Revolution (New York: Oxford University Press 1988), p. 305.

classmate of mine) were waging war against Cuba's economy, intent on destroying the island's sugar mills, tobacco factories, oil refineries, and railroads, along with other targets. By 1958, even the United States, which had provided Batista with nearly unqualified support through most of the 1950s, had decided that he had become a liability. Thus, in March, the United States imposed an arms embargo on Cuba, which severely demoralized the Cuban army and the rest of Batista's supporters, including organized crime families from the United States.

By Jan. 1, 1959, Fidel Castro and his communist party allies had emerged victorious. Thereafter, Cuba's growing political and economic ties to the Soviet Union led to a break in U.S.-Cuban diplomatic relations. Many Americans were alarmed that Communism had gained a foothold just 90 miles from our shores. When Castro seized over $1 billion in U.S. properties, President Eisenhower cut off almost all exports to the island and severely reduced its sugar quota.

But Castro didn't go away. He remained as a formidable challenge to President Kennedy. JFK was an immensely complex and contradictory politician. Intelligent, cultured, and charming, he was also a scrappy Irish fighter, and an implacable foe of the "Red Menace." In an effort to overthrow Castro, JFK gave limited support to a plan that Ike had initiated. The so-called "Bay of Pigs" invasion was carried out by Cuban exiles in April of 1961. Castro's trouncing of the CIA-trained invaders was a huge embarrassment for Kennedy. The setback in the campaign against communism taught JFK a lesson. Half-assed schemes weren't going to get the job done.

Emboldened by his triumph, Castro next permitted the Soviets to set up secret missile bases in Cuba.

The missiles were armed with nuclear warheads and were capable of hitting cities throughout the western hemisphere. Kennedy responded forcefully, taking the nation to the brink of nuclear warfare with the Soviet Union.

Eisenhower had acted decisively to keep communism out of our hemisphere. His administration had been successful in its first effort to rid Latin America of a suspected communist national leader. In 1954 it quite easily arranged the overthrow of Jacobo Arbenz Guzmán, a leftist nationalist who was the elected president of Guatemala. Arbenz was not a self-proclaimed communist, but his wife, Maria Vilanova, was, and communists held important positions in his government.

Under Arbenz, Guatemala had shifted dramatically leftward and had developed close ties to the Soviet Union. Ike's secretary of state, John Foster Dulles, and CIA director, Allen Dulles, were hardline anti-communist brothers, who became convinced that Arbenz was little more than a stooge for the Soviets. According to the "Domino Theory," a governing assumption shaping Latin American-U.S. relations at the time, if Guatemala fell to the "Reds," the remainder of Central America might fall as well.

Arbenz was a champion of agrarian reform. After he seized some of the lands of the U.S.-owned United Fruit Company, which owned vast banana-growing holdings in Guatemala's lowlands, the Dulles duo was infuriated. The compensation that Arbenz offered to United Fruit was based on the company's own undervalued estimates of its lands' worth for purposes of taxation. Arbenz offered $627,572 in bonds as compensation. The United States countered with a demand of nearly $16 million for the seized United Fruit lands.

Suspecting that a U.S. military intervention in his country was imminent, Arbenz ordered a shipment of small arms from Eastern Europe. The Czech weapons arrived in Puerto Barrios in May, 1954. Their arrival was the triggering incident for a unilateral intervention by the United States, whose CIA had been training a few hundred Guatemalan exiles under the leadership of Colonel Carlos Castillo Armas. From their Honduran headquarters, the U.S.-directed exiles invaded Guatemala on June 18, 1954. Guatemala's army was unwilling to resist the U.S.-backed invaders and Arbenz saw the need to step down.

Ike had won, but the United States' overthrow of Arbenz came to symbolize for many Guatemalans the nature of Yankee imperialism. Thereafter and throughout Guatemala III's Peace Corps service, the country was in the grip of the political right, which did the bidding of the big landowners and the foreign investors.

The most tragic reality associated with Guatemalan history in the wake of Group III's departure from the country in 1965 was the brutal and systematic onslaught against human rights. Historians Thomas E. Skidmore and Peter H. Smith sum up the calamity:

> Paramilitary death squads, most notoriously *Mano Blanco* ('White Hand') and *Ojo por Ojo* ('Eye for an Eye'), carried on a murderous campaign against political dissenters. No fewer than 80,000 people were killed or 'disappeared' between the 1960s and the 1990s. The

government bore at least indirect responsibility for these killings, but worldwide protests did not bring much respite.[2]

My wife, Pat, and I knew several of the men who later "disappeared" from our Peace Corps village of Comalapa during those tragic years. Two of them were sons of Don Francisco Telón, the unselfish and conscientious translator/spark plug who rendered Pat's Spanish into Cakchiquel, the Indian language spoken by her women's circle.

Back in 1962, JFK had risked nuclear war by setting up a naval blockade aimed at halting Soviet military shipments to Castro. Thankfully, Nikita Khruschev backed down and decided not to challenge the line Kennedy had drawn. JFK also reinforced our Guantanamo base, compelling the Russians to dismantle their bases in Cuba. Kennedy had stood toe to toe with the Soviets, courting disaster, but, fortunately, they had backed down. Few Americans at the time really appreciated the gravity of the Cuban Missile Crisis. The spunky Irish Catholic president had his way, but Castro was still at the helm in Cuba and he continued his efforts to subvert Latin America. JFK and later Lyndon Johnson responded by invigorating U.S. military cooperation with the 21 member nations making up the Organization of American States.

Kennedy was also faced with communist challenges in Berlin, Laos, and Vietnam. His responses were predictable. On the one hand, he was convinced that the communists could be beaten at their game of fomenting insurgencies among the

---

2   Thomas E. Skidmore and Peter H. Smith, *A*
America, 3rd ed (New York: Oxford University Press, 1

oppressed. Thus, he approved a $19 million budget increase to fund the training of three thousand additional "Special Forces," the celebrated "Green Berets," who specialized in counterinsurgency and unconventional warfare. The mission of the Special Forces would be facilitated by young Americans living and working among humble people throughout the world to win their hearts and minds and make it unlikely that they would join communist insurgencies.

Peace Corps volunteers would help keep the Third World, as it is known today, free of Reds.

Kennedy's executive order setting up the Peace Corps made it clear that its volunteers would bear no resemblance to the all-too-common arrogant Yankee abroad. "They will live at the same level as the citizens of the countries which they are sent to, doing the same work, eating the same food, speaking the same language," he wrote in the order. Kennedy had the requisite charm, wit, intelligence — in a word, charisma — to ensure that his Peace Corps would find no shortage of inspired recruits, both young and old.

At the time I was recruited, I was a first-semester graduate student majoring in history at the University of Wisconsin-Madison. My courses were more challenging and demanding than I had ever imagined. I yearned to lay aside the books and "go bush," as the Australians say. I wanted travel, adventure, physical and mental challenges, and (though it may sound phony to present-day American readers) practical service to humanity. In the process, I could do my part to halt the spread of communism. I was, more than I realized, a product of the Cold War mentality. Peace Corps recruiters, then combing my campus, awakened my interest in JFK's brain-child. Service in remote Shangri-La sounded like the perfect, even justifiable, escape.

Ironically, a novel that I had read during the holiday break before I began my first semester of graduate study had stirred my blood. The Ugly American, a best seller of the day, had sold over five million copies. Written by Eugene Burdick and William Lederer, it was fiction purportedly "based on fact." Earlier, it had left a deep impact on both President Eisenhower and Senator Kennedy. Its simple stories made the point that arrogant Americans abroad were antagonizing people throughout the world, whereas the shrewd communists were winning their hearts and minds, particularly in Sarkhan, a fictionalized Vietnam. The two American heroes in the novel personified the virtues and techniques of model Peace Corps volunteers. They lived and worked among the peasants, helping them to solve their own problems and brighten their cheerless lives by relying on American ingenuity and joie de vivre. The book was a prime motivator for my decision to join the Peace Corps.

The next step would be to persuade Pat to join with me. She was also a student, though an undergrad, at UW-Madison. She was scheduled to receive her bachelor's degree in the spring of 1963. We were to be married on June 22 of that year. My task was to convince her to "go native" after taking off her wedding gown.

I should not have been concerned; Pat has always been more adventurous than I. Even today when our grandchildren want to go on the scariest rides in the amusement park, it is Pat who accompanies them.

I'm glad she was so easily convinced. Our Peace Corps service together helped ensure a long-lasting marriage. Its forty-eight-year duration often mystifies people. Pat and I are completely different people.

She is effervescent and extroverted. I am taciturn and introverted. She functions best when dealing with a dozen issues simultaneously. I can only manage one thing at a time. These differences enable us to complement one another and work together as a more encompassing whole.

I am certain that our Peace Corps service bound us together and convinced us that we could handle almost any challenge or inconvenience together. In the Guatemalan village of Comalapa, we lived in an adobe building with a dirt floor, no hot water, intermittent electricity, and an infant (Susie) to care for. Pat was magnificent in her uncomplaining adjustments to the inconveniences and lack of amenities. I love her all the more for her pluck. Everything Pat and I have done together since our Peace Corps service has been a cake walk.

I SEEM TO RECALL

By Bernie Engel

During our Peace Corps training, several of the guys had trouble getting releases from their draft boards. My own experience was somewhat unique.

In 1963, male volunteers who were subject to the draft (those 18 to 26 who did not have deferments) had to get permission from their draft boards to leave the country. The legislation creating the Peace Corps specifically provided that Peace Corps service would not be a substitute for military duty and would not relieve males from their selective service obligations. I believe President Kennedy made that concession to get support from Republicans and others in Congress who worried that the Peace Corps would have a negative impact on the armed forces.

Before leaving for New Mexico, we males were instructed to contact our draft boards and get written permission to leave the country for the two-year period of our service.

I lived in a close-in suburb of Cleveland called Cleveland Heights. My draft board covered much of the city of Cleveland, which at that time was a predominantly blue-collar town with a significant African-American population, and a small sliver of Cleveland Heights, which was predominantly white-collar and white. The draft board rarely had a problem meeting its quotas, though the majority of draftees were poor and black.

The draft board was a place that young men like me were told to avoid, the theory being that if the board saw a reasonably well-off, healthy white kid in the flesh, the temptation to draft him then and there would be overwhelming.

My problem was how to convince the board to give me permission to leave the country without actually going there and presenting evidence that I was joining the Peace Corps and was not a sneaky suburban malingerer who simply wanted to avoid the draft. The fact that I WAS a sneaky suburban malingerer who wanted to avoid the draft simply complicated matters.

I decided to call the board for information on how to obtain permission to leave the country. I was put through to a woman who sounded as if she were in her twenties (about my age) and who had apparently never heard of the Peace Corps. She asked me what it was and what it did. Well, I put on a performance unlike any I had done before or probably since.

Had you been a fly on the wall and listened to my description of PCV duties and training, you would have thought we were all part Rambo, part Albert Schweitzer and part Mother Theresa.

The woman thought this was a wonderful pursuit for a young man and asked me where I would be serving. For some reason, I knew Guatemala was not the right answer. Chances were she had never heard of the place and that might make her suspicious of everything I had told her up to that point. So with my eyes firmly on the heavens above I said VIETNAM. She gasped. She had heard of the place and thought they needed all the help they could get to keep the communists out. She said there should be no problem providing me with the permission I needed. All I needed to do was come down to the board and pick it up.

I explained I would be happy to do that but I was getting over a bout of dengue fever and could she just mail it to me. She said yes and I exhaled.

So, unlike some of my fellow trainees, I went through training without worrying about my draft board.

THE CAST OF CHARACTERS AT NMSU

By Bernie Engel

Most of the kids in my high-school graduating class were the sons and daughters (or grandsons and granddaughters) of eastern European Jewish immigrants who had managed to realize the American dream. Some were professionals, but most had succeeded in business or trade. In my father's case, it was the delicatessen business.

I had left the Cleveland area only once, as a 15-year-old sent as a chaperone when my soon-to-be brother-in-law took my 18-year-old sister to Ottumwa, Iowa, to meet his family. A foreign excursion for me and my friends was driving to Cleveland's Little Italy for a pizza with pepperoni (my first excursion into the wonderful world of pork!).

Such background will help you appreciate what it was like to meet people who wore sandals (*huaraches*), used words like "bitchin" and ate "veggies." People who were tanned year 'round and enjoyed running in the early morning in the desert. In fact, people who thought the endless brown barren countryside around Las Cruces was beautiful. As you might have guessed, these were the trainees from that foreign country called southern California. To be sure, I'd heard of surfers but I had never actually met one. I wasn't even sure they existed outside of Beach Boy album liners.

Dave Siebert (apologies, Dave) was the archetype. He was tan, wore the sandals, ran every morning, and always headed for the veggies in the cafeteria line. If something was good, it was "bitchin." I forget the word for bad things. He was from another planet! There were others from that foreign land, but he stood out.

In addition, there were the trainees who had actually accomplished things in their young lives. Jay Jackson (from somewhere almost as exotic as southern California — Oregon!) had been some kind of mucky-muck in something called World University Service. I remember trying to find out from him just what this organization did without sounding totally stupid. From the looks he gave me, I'm not sure I succeeded.

My roommate, Chuck Davenport, was from Texas. Of course, he had to be a dumb redneck. Weren't all people who talked that way dumb rednecks?

And there were many others — Schwartz, Mary, Anne, Norma, Ramona, Tim, Bryce, Steve, Ozella and even, wonder of wonders, MARRIED people. It took a while, but I eventually did learn that they were all "bitchin" and accomplished in their own ways (even me) and nice and friendly and a joy to be around. It slowly sank in that we were all in the same boat and whatever prejudices we brought with us had to be checked at the door.

THE MOUNTAIN'S FORMIDABLE CHASM

By Marcia K. Lang

Technically it wasn't a "mountain" we had to conquer during our Peace Corps training in Las Cruces, NM. However, for many of us, the Organ Mountains were daunting. We all came from different backgrounds and my upbringing had not included demanding sport challenges. When I heard about the month-long grueling obstacles we would face during training in Puerto Rico, I secretly dreaded what was ahead.

My brother and sister-in-law invited me for a farewell dinner the night before I was scheduled to leave for Puerto Rico. The main course was snails, succulently prepared and smothered in garlic cloves, a delicacy I had never sampled. They thought they were preparing me for the jungle, yet I knew my knapsack would never be stocked with snail grabbers.

When I returned home that night there was a telegram waiting for me on the kitchen table, curtly informing me not to report for training in Puerto Rico. The training had been canceled due to an outbreak of dengue fever. I couldn't imagine what the fever could be like. I'd never heard of it, but I came down with a dreadful bout in Sri Lanka 12 years later. It was horrific. I couldn't decide *how* to get out of my comfortable, though drenched bed, let alone on which side. I lay in bed in a dark room, with the drapes drawn, because I couldn't tolerate bright sunlight. When my raging fever of 104 degrees subsided two weeks later, the simplest tasks were impossible. I couldn't pick out an outfit from my organized closet. I can't imagine how I could have functioned with crippling indecisiveness in the unfamiliar jungle.

When our group finally arrived in Las Cruces, our trainers were undaunted by the fact that our schedules had to accommodate the "jungle experiences" that we had missed in Puerto Rico. The drown-proofing and the mountain climbing would be slipped into our already overflowing weekends. An underlying, though rarely-mentioned fear, hovered about us, like an unwelcome guest. If we didn't make the grade, we knew we would be "selected out" and sent back home. That fear crept insidiously into our conversations and even occupied our silent thoughts.

I'd taken life-saving courses in high school, so the drown-proofing was no problem for me. The mountain-climbing weekend finally arrived and was broken down into separate challenges. Traversing the intimidating canyon was first. Scrambling up the rocks and rappelling down another side was second. The "mountain men" had rigged a ridiculous-looking rope across the canyon, which we were supposed to glide along to the other side. We would be upside-down, of course. Feet looped over the rope, I inched my way towards the other side, praying that no one would notice my uncontrollable trembling. We were equipped with thick gloves to protect our hands, but I don't remember how I managed to successfully hold onto the rope. My strength and endurance must have been fueled by fear. If I didn't make it across, I faced two options: a gruesome end in the bowels of the treacherous canyon, or a dead-end ticket back to Pennsylvania, to "Dreary Erie," the "Mistake on the Lake."

Traversing occupied all of Saturday. If I'd known what awaited me on Sunday I would have gladly boarded any bus for home. Generally, I volunteer for new opportunities, leading the initial ranks. But as I watched my colleagues struggle to climb the mountain, I regretted my impulsiveness. That Sunday will always be written with indelible CAPITAL RED LETTERS in my memory. The more competitive, agile ones in our group scrambled up the rocks in no time, like a casual stroll in the park. The others tried so hard I doubted I could ever get a foothold. I shrank to the end of the line, terrified.

Maybe it was the fear of facing my parents and friends or having to admit that I couldn't climb the rocks that finally infused me with a sudden surge of energy. My hands magically melded with the first rock, the second cooperated, and then the third joined the ranks. Conquering the mountain filled me with a new bravado. Bruising my whole body against the jagged rocks, I inched my way to the top, like a tortured moth. Breathless, I fluttered about as I viewed those below me, wondering how they would discover their own untapped forces. Those of us who lacked the innate ability to scramble up and over the rocks were forced to draw on unfamiliar inner strengths.

My new-found bravado slipped away as I evaluated the next challenge — jumping across a crevice that appeared to be 12 feet wide, but was probably more like two or three. Great distances separated those of us who were now at the end of the line. No one was there to cheer me on or offer encouragement. Anyone still below me had to be as terrified as I was. Every vista down revealed rugged, uncompromising rocks that could slice me to shreds. After an eternity, I closed my eyes in fear and blindly jumped.

Paul Duffy, one of our instructors, pulled me out of my trance as he shouted to me and told me to get suited up. I took a deep breath because that meant I was to put a belt around my waist and attach myself to him with a gizmo called a carabiner. Paul remained anchored into the top of the mountain. I was supposed to soar down the mountainside. Wow! That sounded sensational. When I took off, it felt like I was soaring. I looked down to see how far I had to go. A third of the way, a narrow ledge jutted out.

"Fine," I thought. "I'll just rest there, catch my breath, and then glide to the bottom like a magnificent bird." The moment I hit the ledge, I screamed. "PAUL! PAUL! LOOK, MY CARABINER BROKE!" Terrified, I held the pieces in my hands, trembling at the thought of crashing down the jagged rocks and falling to my death.

41

It seemed like I'd already died three times that day, and now I was literally at the end of my rope. Paul screamed: "Well, fix it, damn it! JUST FIX IT!"

Furious, I screamed back, "How? How CAN I fix it?" I held the pieces, fearing I'd never find a way down the mountainside. Maybe I wasn't meant to go to Guatemala. My father had told me I'd made a stupid decision. I could hear his voice: "You want to give up everything you have to go to Guatemala?" Perhaps he was right. Dreary Erie was starting to look better and better from my precarious vantage point on the mountain.

"Hey!" Paul shouted, trying to bring me back to the task at hand. "Fix the damn thing now and get down this ____ mountain!"

His screaming brought me back to the moment, but I continued gaping at the pieces. "How do I fix it?" I shouted back.

"Just take the damn pieces and fit them back together." Then I heard a slight change in his voice. "You CAN do it, Marcia, I know you can!"

I thought the ledge was shrinking. My feet hurt and my knees shivered and pounded against the rocks. Fear rippled through my body, through all the muscles I hadn't used before.

I started dreaming of home, my luxurious deep-green bathtub. The hot steaming water would soothe my aching body. It overflowed with bubbly suds that smelled like my Grandmother's lilac bushes. I closed my eyes . . .

"Marcia! Hey — have ya got it together yet? The sun's goin' down soon!"

A slight chill brushed the back of my neck. I was bone tired, but talked myself into focusing on my belt, slowly fitting the pieces together. Somehow, I managed to clip the belt back around my middle. I grabbed the swinging rope and felt the tension Paul was putting on it from above. The tension connected us and calmed me. My fear slithered down the rocks and disappeared into a crevice. I willed it to leave me.

Next thing I knew I was touching solid earth, grateful I'd survived. I didn't wonder about the others until much later. How had they fared? Had they survived? I was thankful to climb into the bus knowing it would carry me back to the dorm. There would be no luxurious bath suds, no lilac-scented sheets, not even a steaming pot of tea. However, there was a deep satisfaction that the mountain hadn't conquered me. Dreary Erie plummeted into the mountain's yawning crevice.

A HARD DAY'S WORK

By Norma Wilder Benevides

In Las Cruces I had a complex about being the youngest member of Guatemala III — always being left behind to be babysat when the group went to unwind at a bar after a rough week of training.

My fears were real. When I saw the gulch we had to traverse in our mountain climbing experience, I nearly fainted!

It was all I could do to imagine myself actually going across it, but I knew I could not watch anyone else go and wait for my turn. So it was not out of bravery that I heard myself blurt out, "I want to go first!" It was just the opposite.

Sure enough, they were happy to have a sucker and the next thing I knew I was being strapped in and hanging from the line. There were two guys on the other side of the gulch waiting to pull me over, but the line was not taut enough, and my own weight made me stop midway across.

Three hundred feet below, I saw an ambulance. That was my darkest moment. And then, everyone yelled, "Don't look down!"

The two guys struggled to pull me over, and of course, afterward, they tightened the rope.

Everyone else sailed across with no problem, except for Marcia Lang whose rope clip somehow came open. I remember how nervous and sweaty the two rope pullers were, anxiously calling to Marcia to be careful, to go slowly and to pull herself up until she could latch the clip on the rope once again. That was a tense time, much worse than my weight problem.

I was so glad I had gone first to protect myself!

WHY I JOINED THE PEACE CORPS

By Carolyn Plage

I had been raised to believe that it was my job to help make the world a better place. Much of my life was lived in a small town an hour north of New York City, among middle class "white folks," whose biggest differences were whether they went to the Lutheran Church, the Dutch Reformed Church, or the Roman Catholic Church.

Three years at New York University in Manhattan introduced me to foreign-exchange students and to the cosmopolitan atmosphere of the city. My first year at NYU (after a hated freshman year at an all-girls college in Pennsylvania), I campaigned for Richard Nixon for president, was active in Young Americans for Freedom and was hooked on Ayn Rand's writings and thinking.

That phase passed and by 1963, I was intrigued with John F. Kennedy and his plea, "Ask not what your country can do for you — ask what you can do for your country." I also liked the idea of fleeing my small home town and seeing the world.

Two college friends applied to the Peace Corps and encouraged me to do the same. They didn't make it. I did. I turned down my acceptance to grad school in Albany. Having a good background in Spanish from high school and college, and thinking I'd like to see the fjords of southern Chile, I made that country my first choice. When I received my assignment to Guatemala, I had to check the map, but I was ready to go.

JFK, SIGNING UP AND PC TRAINING

By Patricia (Pat) Garity Smits and Dave Smits

Pat:

Forty-eight years ago! What's amazing is, I can remember some of the events as if they happened yesterday.

Left to my own devices I would not have "signed up" and wouldn't have given it a second thought if the Peace Corps hadn't responded favorably to my application. Back in '63, I was a full-time student at the University of Wisconsin in Madison, also working full time at a job I loved. My husband, Dave, was completing his master's degree. I thought our lives were planned out for the next few years. So what happened?

I don't remember our first conversation about the Peace Corps, but I do know that Dave was the one who suggested it. The Peace Corps came to UW to recruit volunteers. Why they wanted young, inexperienced, naïve men and women (the politically correct way to refer to boys and girls), with no life skills and no practical experience, to send around the world to represent the United States is anybody's guess. What I do remember is being dragged out of bed after working most of the night to take a language proficiency test.

As a Midwesterner, I came to the Peace Corps by a circuitous route. I was born to a political family and raised in a small Wisconsin town between Milwaukee and Madison. Of course, successful politicians in that part of the state, my father among them, were all Republicans. Unlike most of the Irish who immigrated to this country, my father's family had come through Canada and settled in Wisconsin. Like many small towns in the state, mine had been settled by Germans. There were only a few families of other nationalities and most had lived there for generations. The only diversity was religious. The two largest churches were the Lutheran and the Roman Catholic, on hills a block apart. Although I didn't realize it, we were outsiders in some ways. My father and mother had grown up elsewhere in Wisconsin and had come to Jefferson as young single adults to pursue job opportunities.

As a child I didn't think much about my parents' different family backgrounds. My maternal Swedish relatives were reserved. But my father came from a large gregarious Irish-Catholic family. They constantly debated any timely issue. At the time, I didn't appreciate the fact that my father raised me just as he would have raised a son — to be a hard-working, independent thinker — not a girl with gender limitations. My paternal grandfather was killed in an industrial accident when my father, the oldest boy in a family of eleven children, was only twelve years old. His mother, a stalwart woman, kept the entire family together in a time before social security or any other safety net. My father had a profound respect for his mother and his church. He was a natural politician who started out as a Democrat, but realized that the only way to get elected in our rural county was to run on the Republican ticket. Actually, the only contested elections were the primaries.

I share my background to explain the impact that John F. Kennedy (that handsome young Irish politician with the strange way of speaking) had when he campaigned in Wisconsin. Politics were heatedly discussed in my family and among the adults in my world. It was apparent to me at an early age that I would never embrace conservative political views. The civil rights movement had a big impact on me. I wanted to go into the South to register voters and march against segregation. But my father forbade me from going because I was too young — and it was too dangerous.

Even though I grew up in a lily-white town, the injustice of segregation and discrimination against blacks and other minorities offended me. When young, I had traveled by car through the South and stopped at restaurants where blacks (Negroes) were not served. I had seen water fountains labeled "white only." There were no black families living in my town. As kids we played down at the Rock River, a favorite fishing spot for black people who came out from Milwaukee. I remember them being friendly and sharing their bait with us. That was the limit of my contact with blacks, except for an experience I had while working at a local restaurant. One day, a black man entered the restaurant and when I walked to the front where he was standing, he asked if he could buy a cup of coffee. I asked him to join the other customers, but he seemed surprised. Apparently, he expected only to be able to buy coffee to take out. I was too naïve to realize that a black man walking into a restaurant in small-town Wisconsin would be concerned about the reception he would get.

Into my sheltered provincial world came a tidal wave of change. It probably started with the music. Instead of Sinatra or traditional Country music the juke box at the local hang-out in my home town rocked with Elvis, Jerry Lee and black groups. Even lectures by the nuns at the Catholic boarding school I attended were unable to hold back the tide. But let me get back to Wisconsin politics of the 1960s. Midwestern voters who voted for Democrats favored Hubert Humphrey, then a U.S. Senator from Minnesota. It was Humphrey who introduced the idea of the Peace Corps, though he had another name for his plan. I was a Humphrey supporter, though I was too young to vote.

I don't recall how I learned that John Kennedy would be speaking at UW shortly before the Wisconsin primary. The first time he came to campus he spoke in the Music Hall. The small auditorium was packed. I still remember exactly where I stood. I don't recall his speech, but I do recall the memorable way he answered questions after his brief speech. I had probably listened to hundreds of political speeches in my young life, but I never heard anyone as mesmerizing as Kennedy. He randomly took questions from the audience, answered each question, then pointed back to the questioner and asked if the question had been fully answered. He actually answered rather than responding with political double talk. He handled all questions, including the attempts to undermine his campaign with religious scare tactics. Religion was a significant factor in politics at that time. Kennedy had an uphill battle as an Irish Catholic easterner up against Hubert Humphrey, a beloved elder statesman from Minnesota. But JFK made at least one convert that night — me.

Kennedy's impact was fresh in my mind when Dave suggested we apply for the Peace Corps.

I don't recall thinking much about the Peace Corps or how much time elapsed between the application and acceptance. I didn't bother to mention it to my parents. They were unhappy enough with my choices — including getting married. My father believed that women could have wonderful careers — as long as they were single.

When I next heard from my father, he was less than pleased. His phone was ringing off the hook with calls from the local banker and other businessmen in my home town (population 3,000) because FBI agents were asking questions about me all over town. An FBI visit to small-town Wisconsin was not a daily or even yearly event. It set the tongues a-wagging: "What in the world has that Garity girl done now?" Rumors must have circulated through the small-town gossip mill for months. Apparently, the FBI never found out about my teenage antics (that today would land kids in juvenile court) because I was accepted.

I don't recall whether Dave or I received the acceptance letter first. What I do recall is that we were each selected, but assigned to serve in different countries! I'm not sure how we convinced the Peace Corps that assigning us to different countries was not acceptable or the process we had to go through to be assigned to the *same* country, but it finally happened. The telegram arrived the night before we were leaving to begin the initial Peace Corps training stint in Puerto Rico and just after we loaded the last of our boxes in the car to take to my parents' home before our flight.

Dave:

The first hint for Pat and me that the Peace Corps bureaucracy had not yet mastered its affairs came when each of us got a telegram informing us of the country where we would serve in Latin America. One of us was to be sent to Guatemala; the other, to Colombia. We balked. In the end, we were assigned to the same country.

The cancellation of our training in Puerto Rico left us unemployed, homeless and unstable. Our next communication from the Peace Corps was a phone call from Las Cruces, NM, inquiring as to why we had not arrived at the state university.

Peace Corps told us to get ourselves to Las Cruces pronto and to foot the bill for our own transportation. But intermittent employment since being left jobless had put us in financial distress. We were forced to wait until Peace Corps provided vouchers for our flight to El Paso.

Pat:

Our training was supposed to begin in Puerto Rico in August, 1963. Dave and I were living in a one-room "apartment" on the second floor of a private home next to Madison's Vilas Park Zoo. Only people who have lived in tiny New York studio apartments could appreciate just how small it was. The sofa bed was at one end of the room and the "kitchen" at the other. Our legs hung off the bed and there was not enough room to walk around the bed when it was open. Stairs in the hallway led to the attic. The only way not to disturb Dave when I came home from work and had to study was to sit on the attic stairs. But we thought we were incredibly lucky to even have an apartment in Madison. Married student housing on campus was at a premium and the waiting list was impossible. Single students drove up the prices because they could pack three or four or more students into a small apartment. We thought ourselves lucky to have found a place to live, even if it wasn't as large as my horses' stalls at home. We kept the windows open to survive the summer heat without air conditioning. Living next to the zoo with all the intoxicating animal smells was better training for the Peace Corps than I could have imagined.

Training was scheduled in Puerto Rico near the end of the summer. Dave was working full time that summer at Borden's Dairy, loading refrigerator trucks, and I was attending summer school and working full time. We quit our jobs and gave our landlord notice just before our scheduled training in Puerto Rico. We had just finished packing our meager possessions, which we were going to store in my parents' basement, when the infamous telegram arrived. I vividly remember sitting on the steps to read it. It was some last-minute instruction about the training in Puerto Rico, where we were scheduled to fly the next day. Instead, we learned that training in Puerto Rico had been cancelled because of an outbreak of dengue fever. The training in New Mexico wasn't scheduled to start for three weeks.

Now what? We were homeless and jobless. We actually thought we might end up living out of our car or sleeping in the zoo.

Dave saved the day because of his friendship with the owners of the corner store across from our apartment. I didn't realize how often he went there for snacks while I was working or at school. (Frankly, I think they were disappointed when they learned we were leaving because he was their best, or one of their best, customers.) When he told them that our Peace Corps training had been postponed and that we were about to be homeless, they invited us to look at the nearby vacant furnished apartment on the second floor of an elderly woman's home. I don't recall if our benefactor (life saver) even charged us rent. What I do recall is that the apartment was a tremendous improvement over our prior apartment and it would be the best housing we would have for many years. Instead of moving our possessions to my parents' home, we moved a block away. To support ourselves until training began, Dave became a day laborer, taking whatever jobs were available out of the local Manpower office. I worked for my father, driving from Madison daily.

Dave:

After finishing my work each day at Borden's Dairy, I returned to our tiny apartment only to find Pat away at her job. Left to fend for myself, I filled my time with creative and productive activity: I ate. The corner grocery across the street was my first step on a long journey toward corpulence, still ongoing. But my visits brought a payoff. While buying my usual morning coffee and pastry, I revealed that our Puerto Rican training had just been cancelled and we were now homeless.

The grocer's response was instantaneous. To this day I remain convinced that his fear of insolvency, should I depart the neighborhood, galvanized him into action. He told me that a regular customer in the next block had an unrented apartment in her home. Pat and I moved into new digs barely 100 yards from my critical food source. I found employment as a day-laborer at Manpower, Inc. until we left for Las Cruces.

Three weeks later, we flew into the border city of El Paso, Texas and, while waiting for the Greyhound to Las Cruces, we strolled the city's main plaza where we experienced an overpowering sensation of being outsiders. We heard only Spanish spoken and the people bore little resemblance to our Midwestern selves. The food, clothing, and music were unfamiliar. It was our first taste of the subsequently predicted "culture shock" we'd face in Guatemala. Ironically, it was in our own country.

Pat:

Another hurry up and wait! We settled into our stop-gap apartment after the initial flurry to unpack some essentials. Then we took temporary jobs to earn enough to pay our living expenses until training began. We expected to hear from the Peace Corps about training in New Mexico, but nothing happened. Finally, we received the call — not about transportation arrangements, but about our failure to show up for training! By the time Peace Corps called, Group III had begun training in New Mexico. They had neglected to send us the training schedule or transportation vouchers to get there. When they finally called, they expected us to pay for plane tickets to El Paso, Texas and leave immediately. That almost ended our Peace Corps adventure. We couldn't afford the tickets. Happily, a few days later we received the necessary vouchers and were on our way.

My memory of leaving Madison and arriving in El Paso is still vivid after all these years, not because it was my first plane trip but because it seemed as if we had landed in a foreign country. We killed time in downtown El Paso for a few hours waiting for the bus to Las Cruces. Everyone was speaking Spanish. It really was culture shock.

Other than intensive language training, most of the training didn't make much sense. I recall agriculture training. We needed to know how to make compost, not the differences between types of commercial fertilizer! Mandatory classes about communism were also part of the curriculum since the Cold War was still hanging over us in the early 60s. I don't recall learning anything about nutrition or health care but we did have to know how to tread water.

Treading water test: My big, strong husband almost panicked when he learned that we had to tread water for 60 minutes as part of our training. But it was a snap for me. I had been a life guard and swimming instructor for years, but Dave wasn't much of a swimmer and was sure that he would drown.

Soccer: Sports were included in the training. We played mixed volley ball and the women played either soccer or field hockey. My most vivid memory of group sports was playing soccer/field hockey when Christie McReynolds unintentionally knocked me down. I'm not sure that she knocked me out, but I know I saw stars. I doubt I would recall the incident if I had not been pregnant.

Mountain climbing: I thought it was thrilling. My only concern was whether it posed any risk to a pregnant woman.

In Mexico, after an endless bus trip from Chihuahua, we arrived in Casas Grandes. Our local contact was a Catholic priest. We visited Colonia Juárez and Colonia Dublán, exile communities founded by Mormons when polygamy was banned in the United States. There was a striking contrast between the public school attended by non-Mormon children and the up-to-date Mormon schools.

My early pregnancy was unremarkable except during the trip to Casas Grandes. Trying to keep breakfast down was impossible, especially because Dave insisted on my drinking milk. I couldn't even look at runny eggs and trying to keep warm unpasteurized milk down was impossible. Of course, we also had to make sure that no one suspected I was pregnant.

One memory of the Mexico training was a party at the local Padre's house. He was very proud of his small vineyard and of his homemade wine. We all wanted to be polite, but the wine tasted terrible. I knew more than a sip would be impossible, but I could easily exchange glasses with Dave so no one would realize that I wasn't drinking. I wasn't the only one who couldn't drink the wine. Soon Dave was exchanging his empty glass for full ones from several people. By the time we left — riding in the back of the Padre's pickup truck — Dave was so drunk he could barely stand. I don't know if he remembers the ride back to the hotel!

Kennedy's assassination occurred during our training. Each of us has painful memories of that tragic day. I have never met anyone who can't remember precisely what they were doing when they heard that Kennedy had been shot. We all hung on every word from Dallas, hoping and praying that the news would not be what we dreaded.

Dave:

I have enduring memories of that pickup-truck ride. It was the most noteworthy personal humiliation of our training experience in Casas Grandes.

More important, it was dramatically clear from her bouts with morning sickness that Pat was pregnant. I felt it was my duty to provide her a healthy diet, meaning plenty of fresh milk. Warm unpasteurized milk was an inexhaustible supply. But Pat couldn't hold it down and it was too risky. Cold pasteurized milk was a necessity, but no living Mexican had ever actually seen it.

A Roman Catholic priest had been acting as our channel into the Mexican communities to which we were assigned. The good padre seemed to enjoy the company of North Americans and cordially invited us to a reception at his home. There he proudly served his homemade wine, made from grapes grown in his own vineyard. Most in our group found the wine undrinkable, excessively sweet. I, owing to my mother's admonitions to finish what I had been served, quickly downed my glass. When Pat saw that, she rushed to exchange her full glass for my empty one. Other guests observed Pat's maneuver and followed her example. By departure time I had become gloriously drunk.

We piled into the back of a pickup for the long ride back to our hotel. With my head hanging over the tailgate, disgorging my guts, I could not have inspired much respect for "gringos" among the locals. My dear wife and the other volunteers were too convulsed with laughter to comfort me.

MOTIVATION

By Tim Kraft

The recruiter who came to my college was a young, well-spoken and persuasive individual. His name was John F. Kennedy.

To back up a little, as a freshman at Dartmouth, I joined the Young Democrats Club, an endangered species on that mostly conservative campus. An even smaller sub-group was Students for Kennedy, of which I became chairman (the other guy lost the coin toss).

I conspired with our faculty advisor, an affable history professor, to get the college to extend a speaking invitation to Senator Kennedy. That was January of 1960 and he had just announced his candidacy.

New Hampshire held the first primary on March 8, one of only 16 primaries nationwide at that time. It seemed a good event for both the college and the candidate. He accepted and we had a date in February.

When Kennedy arrived, Professor MacLaine and I greeted him in the foyer of the auditorium. I was introduced as his campus coordinator and a lengthy and meaningful conversation ensued. It went exactly like this:

Kraft: "Welcome to Hanover, Senator, thanks for coming."

Kennedy, after a quick handshake, no smile: "There are an awful lot of Nixon signs out there."

Oh well. I escorted him to the stage and took my aisle seat, third row.

That rebuke didn't cool my jets. I liked him and thought that sometime in the future I would like to work in his administration.

And besides, I had just gotten a fine lesson on one facet of political advance work.

SECTION II

PEACE
CORPS
WRITERS

SERVICE IN GUATEMALA

A HARD LESSON LEARNED

By Norma Wilder Benevides

The first time I rode down the street in my assigned *barrio* (ward), I saw the local women washing clothes in front of the church, in a barren field with a large *pila* (sink) and just one clothesline. Most of the laundry was strewn over the ground to dry, with only a few pieces on the clothesline.

"Okay," I thought to myself, "the first thing I need to do is to raise funds to buy more clotheslines."

NOT!!

They did not want more clotheslines and I learned a totally new way to wash clothes.

First, they scrubbed the clothes and filled them with as much soap as possible. Then they put them on the ground on purpose, to cake dry, which was a natural bleaching process. After that, the women rinsed the clothes and hung them on the line to dry.

Duh, Norma, they did not want, or need, more clotheslines. Thus, began my education in how to understand living in another culture.

THE BEST OF TIMES/THE WORST OF TIMES

By Charlie Carreras

I had a meeting at my house in Guatemala City with a group of teenagers. At the same time, there was a meeting in the local parish about 10 blocks away that I wanted to attend.

When my meeting ended, I jumped on my bike, a piece of unclaimed property from the city police, given to Jay Jackson, Bill Pierson and me. I hurriedly biked to the other meeting.

The city was repairing the road in front of the church and a manhole cover had been left off. As I flew down the street in pitch darkness, I crashed into that manhole.

I lost five minutes of my life there. Next thing I knew I was at the *bomberos*, the fire department.

The firemen had picked me up and whisked me away to Roosevelt Hospital. The next day, our Peace Corps doctor transferred me to a private clinic where I mended quickly.

For me it's pretty embarrassing to think about even now, but I survived. And, I'm still rushing off to meetings!

There were a lot of experiences that could be classified as my best day in the Peace Corps. One that stands out is the day we left Guatemala and Peace Corps service. I had such mixed feelings about leaving, as we all probably did. I was excited to be going home, to be seeing my family and friends again and to be starting graduate school. At the same time, I was sad to be leaving such a beautiful country and such wonderful people. I had had such a great time and it was coming to an end, as we all knew it would.

While we were waiting in the airport terminal, a group of people I had worked with in my neighborhood came to see me off. Young people from the club where I had worked were there, and people from the neighborhood committee.

I had no idea they would be there and I felt so good that they had come! I still have a picture of all of us in the airport.

It was bittersweet, a day that had to be, as we all moved on to the next stage of our lives.

MY PEACE CORPS EXPERIENCE

By Ginny Moran

I was a senior at Texas Woman's University in Denton, Texas in 1961, and followed with interest the development of the Peace Corps. After graduation, I worked for a year in Austin for a graphic arts company to pay off school debts, then signed up for the Peace Corps and was accepted!

I reported for the required physical and shots (12, I believe) at Langley Air Force Base in San Antonio. I stood in line with two dozen military recruits, all of us carrying our urine samples and waiting our turn for physicals.

I reported for training in Las Cruces, NM with 68 other volunteers assigned to Guatemala. There I learned the language, dress, and culture of the country, and visited the town of General Triasin, Mexico, where I lost all interest in pork as a food source.

After being stuck in crevices while rappelling and belaying in the Organ Mountains, I ripped the sleeve of my best sweatshirt in the slow aerial crossing of a deep gorge. The mishap stopped the momentum that was to carry me at least half-way across the abyss with my eyes shut, but I managed to make it, thanks to the you-can-do-it cheering of fellow volunteers.

As volunteers, we supported one another when the news reached us that President John F. Kennedy had been assassinated. He had developed the Peace Corps idea and was largely responsible for our being in Las Cruces. I headed for the chapel with others and cried. We had lost our leader and were uncertain about the future of his infant Peace Corps and whether it would survive.

Fortunately, we endured and kept his dream alive. After training and a Christmas break, we flew to Guatemala City. There we learned our respective destinations. Three others and I were assigned to, Quezaltepeque, Chiquimula, a six-hour bus trip away along the dusty Pan Am Highway. We had our first view of Quezaltepeque as we descended a steep mountain. The tiny town was deep in a valley surrounded by green mountains. In the center was a small white *iglesia*, or church, surrounded by a plaza. Within the plaza were tiny shops or *tiendas*, a bakery, grocery, drug store, and butcher shop.

The town's leaders were eager to meet the new arrivals. Our first introduction was to the *alcalde,* or mayor, who provided us with a place to live. It was a one-room warehouse across from a school attended by everyone from kindergarten to high school. The warehouse was made of adobe blocks with a clay tile roof. We made dividers of heavy cotton stretched across wooden frames to create four areas for sleeping. Our shower was a garden hose extended from the ceiling on a back porch. We were fortunate to have a *pila* (or sink) for washing and water to boil for drinking.

Working with the townspeople and in schools in Quezaltepeque and surrounding villages, I became convinced that our greatest contribution was to change negative ideas about, and dispel the fear of, Americans. Misconceptions were based on a lack of knowledge and hearsay.

Our first visit to the Indian schools was a major example. Each teacher knew we would be there on a certain day to meet with them and their students, and to see the classes in action. On our first few visits we encountered classrooms with no children. Much later, we learned the reason. The teachers told us that parents kept their children from school on those days because they were afraid Americans were coming to take them away. Some parents even thought we were going to eat their kids.

One Indian school was an exception, since the teacher had explained in advance who Americans were and had hung up a colorful poster of a Pepsodent tooth paste advertisement. The poster showed a smiling blond American girl brushing her teeth. When our group walked into that school, the children cheered and pointed at me (the blond among the *gringos*). I was the Pepsodent girl to them.

We were all like the person in the poster so we were okay.

Just as my introduction to Guatemala was a memorable day, so was the exit. After flying out of Guatemala, I arrived at the airport in Miami with another volunteer. A huge crowd had formed and it was difficult to get through to the luggage area. We joked about "our" greeting, not knowing why the mob was actually there. A huge crowd of mostly teens and college-age youths had formed and were running and screaming. I managed to slow one girl down for a question.

"What's the mob for?" I asked.

"Haven't you heard? The Beatles are arriving!" she responded.

"What are Beatles?" we asked.

With no TV or radios in Quezaltepeque or Tikal, we had no idea what the fuss was about. We had returned during the arrival of the legendary Beatles, on their first trip to the United States. With flights to catch we missed the big event.

MY PEACE CORPS SERVICE

By Bob Keberlein

When I arrived in Chaparron in early 1964, I first worked with its young men who wanted to play soccer but had no equipment. All of them worked long hours planting, weeding and harvesting their meager crops and barely earned enough money to help feed their families. Some played musical instruments or sang, so we started a band and held weekly dances.

Our band had two guitar players, one violinist, one drummer, three guys on the *marimba*, and one young man who made noise with anything handy — an old piece of cow's horn, an old bell or a piece of tin. Once in a while, Chon, the town character, would join us on the *marimba* and vocals. He could sing and play very well. Although our instruments were old and often not quite in tune, our listeners never complained.

The proceeds from these activities provided us with several soccer balls, shoes and uniforms. The uniforms were green and gold. (What would you expect, with a cheesehead from Wisconsin for a "coach?") We played every Sunday afternoon, against regional rivals, and even chartered a bus to take us to the El Salvador border to play. We became very good. In 1965, we were crowned league champions.

As a team, we also completed several projects around town to improve local life. We built a basketball court, capped a pure water source and built latrines.

Of the many memories I have of my Peace Corps days, one stands out. When I arrived in Chaparron, there was no such thing as a hotel or rooming house. The priest in charge of the local parish invited me to stay in his room at the church. Normally, the room sat vacant because he lived in a larger, distant community and came to Chaparron only once or twice a year. The church was maintained by a devout young lady. She often led the faithful in prayer.

One day I heard a knock on my door and opened it to find a man who had come to ask if I would help his village of Los Vivares. His name was Antonio "Tono" Martinez. In 1964, Los Vivares was a tiny village of perhaps 30 or 40 flimsy homes. Most were nothing more than huts made of wood and straw. Everyone lived by planting corn and beans. Most of the inhabitants rented the land they worked. There were no stores. There was no electricity, no medical attention and no school. Water was carried in jugs from a small well more than a kilometer from the village. Every man, woman and child struggled just to stay alive.

Roads were nonexistent. All supplies were brought in and other goods carried out of the village by horse, mule or ox. I remember many trips on my horse over those terrible paths to Los Vivares. At times, I had to get off my horse and pull him over the large boulders that the rains had moved and scattered over the path. There are now paved roads and well-built modern homes in that village.

Of the many difficulties that life presented to the 1960s inhabitants of Los Vivares, the lack of education was the most devastating. The village and its children had no school. There was not one resident who could read or write. Whenever anyone wanted to write a letter, he or she had to travel the seven kilometers to the nearest town, San Manuel Chaparron, just to find someone to read or write a letter for them.

Tono Martinez was the father of 15, the town elder and its unofficial leader. He wanted to build a school so his children could learn to read and write. The town was willing to build the school, but the townspeople needed help to obtain lumber for the roof and some school supplies. Of course, they also needed a teacher.

The day after Tono knocked on my door, I visited his village and spoke with the people. When I spoke with the Minister of Education, I found out that the village actually did have a teacher. The teacher just never showed up because there was no place for him to live or to teach in Los Vivares.

With the help of CARE and a lot of work, we built a two-room school with a small additional room for the teacher's residence.

CARE provided many materials, such as roof beams and *lámina* [layers of wood], tiles for the floors and even educational materials for the students. Villagers provided all the labor and the adobes. After a year and a half of work, we inaugurated the school.

When word got out about the school we had built in Los Vivares, I received petitions from several other villages needing a new or improved school. We built schools in Las Animas, Los Amates and Poza Verde. We built an additional three rooms onto the school in Chaparron. A U.S. program called School-To-School provided funds for the construction.

I wonder if "Keni" Kent (CARE director in Guatemala who doubled as Guatemala III's director our first year) recalls helping us build desks for some of those schools. He employed a unique system of metal frames to which we attached two long pieces of wood to make a desk for four to five students. The same process was used for the seats. Some of those desks are still in use in those schools.

When it became obvious to me that my tour would end before seeing all of these building projects to completion, I requested and was granted permission from the Peace Corps to serve for an additional year. I did not leave Guatemala until more than a year after the departure of most of the Guatemala III Peace Corps volunteers.

In January 1966, I married that devout young lady who maintained the church and led everyone in prayer. With her, I returned to my Wisconsin roots when I left Chaparron in October 1966. We were blessed with two sons. Douglas was born in 1969, and Michael in 1972. Both have had a great impact on life in Chaparron and in Guatemala.

A PEACE CORPS STORY (THAT I THINK ACTUALLY HAPPENED)

By Bernie Engel

All Guatemala III volunteers were within reach by bus, jeep or horseback, except for Tim Kraft and Carol Bellamy, who were stationed in the Petén, a thumb-like appendage sticking out of the top of the country, bordering Mexico and Belize. The Petén is best known for the ancient Mayan ruins of Tikal, perhaps the number-one tourist attraction in Guatemala. Flores is the capital city of Petén and, at least during Guatemala III's time in country, was reachable only by air. That was because of Petén's impenetrable jungle.

Tim was then assigned to Station Elena. He invited Bob and Sue Hetzel and me to join him for a trip through the jungle to a place called Sayaxché. It sounded like fun.

Air service to Flores was provided courtesy of the Guatemalan Air Force (in Spanish, Fuerza Aerea Guatemalteca). There were regularly scheduled flights in FAG DC-3s, which in the early 60s must have been, at minimum, 30 years old, having come into service in the 1930s. The age of the planes, coupled with what we had learned about the Guatemalan government's cavalier attitude about maintenance, made flying in one a genuine adventure.

On our flight to Flores, I visited the flight deck (what we used to call the cockpit) and chatted with the pilots. It was not exactly your normal commercial flight. The plane carried passengers and supplies and we wandered around the airplane at our pleasure. The pilots were a relaxed pair who chatted and smoked as we cruised somewhat lower than I had expected. It soon became clear why when one of the pilots looked out his window and said, "Oh, there's the bend in the river. I think we turn left here." They turned and I scurried to the rear of the aircraft, having heard somewhere that the rear of a plane is the safest place to be in a crash.

We arrived in Flores and made our way to Sta. Elena where Tim had made arrangements for transportation to Sayaxché. We traveled by pickup over the gravel, soon-to-become-mud road, then relied on outboard-motor-driven dugout canoes for movement on the river. Our camping equipment included rifles and shotguns for any nasty snakes we might encounter. (Knowing that made my day!)

Riding in the back of the truck, we encountered a large partially fallen tree limb that blocked the road. Those of us in the back grabbed the branch and lifted it up and over. As I was about to release the branch, I felt a sharp pain in the palm of my hand and saw two small punctures. I looked up at the branch to see what had caused the wound. A thorn? A sharp piece of bark? One of those snakes we were supposed to kill with the shotgun? Or maybe a poisonous bug defending its territory?

My hand began to swell and I broke into a cold sweat. My colleagues looked at my hand and said there was nothing to worry about. Easy for them to say. I was convinced I had little time left to live. Slowly sliding to the floor of the vehicle, I quietly passed out, thinking that dying wasn't so bad. I didn't die. Instead I had to put up with several hours of insults and wisecracks from my companions, who, if they weren't already convinced, now were sure I was the single biggest wimp and drama-queen in Guatemala III.

While gliding along the river and keeping our eyes out for jaguars (hoping against hope that we would see one), we noticed a good-sized iguana sunning itself on a tree limb. I grabbed my rifle (a .22), aimed and fired. What I didn't notice was the fellow behind me who had the same idea and fired at the same time from a distance of five inches from my left ear. I jumped and the iguana fell into the river. We recovered the animal and had him for dinner that night and *yes*, it *did* taste like chicken.

One day as we glided along the river, we turned into a small intersecting stream that led into a small lake. We motored to the shore and found an abandoned encampment. There were water pipes, huts, wash basins, and rusting generators, all surrounding what appeared to be an assembly area. Most curious of all were the shell casings — many, many shell casings. What on earth was this? An abandoned hunting camp? An old archeological camp (with shell casings)? Tim asked one of the Guatemalans if he knew who had been there and the man replied, *"Pues, no se exactamente... unos gringos y cubanos estuvieron aqui un rato."* (Rough translation: "I know exactly what went on here and it involved gringos and Cubans, but if I tell you I may not live to see old age.").

As it turned out, it did involve gringos and Cubans. (Time out for a brief history lesson.) When the decision was made to mount an invasion of Cuba, the CIA was charged with recruiting and training the invasion force. Recruiting was no problem. The large

Cuban-exile community of south Florida was fertile ground. Finding a place to train them was a problem. U.S. military bases were out of the question and the National Park Service was not about to sub-let Yellowstone or any other park. So the CIA turned its eyes south. What country might be willing to turn a blind eye and allow Cubans and U.S. CIA personnel to visit for a while and train for an invasion of a large Caribbean island? Guatemala, that's who. The owners of several large *fincas* [landed estates] were recruited and the Cuban/CIA force moved in to learn the fine art of amphibious landing. How that was possible in the highlands of Guatemala still escapes me.

Any large group (particularly a large military group) is going to contain a certain percentage of troops who are, shall we say, a bit too gung-ho. According to David Wise and Thomas Ross, authors of The Invisible Government, the CIA did not want such psychos involved in the invasion. What to do? Sending them back to Miami was not an option. The solution was to tell those troops they were being selected for a special operation that would require special training. A camp was set up — you guessed it — in the isolated jungle region of the Petén. Risky troops remained there until the final fiasco played out and they were quietly dispersed to Miami and other points *afuera de Cuba* [outside Cuba].

Back to my own adventures. . . . The following day, we traveled along the river and at some point, beached the canoes and started to walk inland. We came upon a clearing and could see, perhaps a hundred yards away, tents and many people, some working at tables, some digging and others just generally busy. We walked to a large tent where men were sitting behind a table.

Now, imagine five or six dirty, unshaven men, a million miles from nowhere, in the middle of the jungle, walking purposefully toward you carrying rifles and shotguns. As we approached the tent, one man finally looked up and saw us coming. His eyes grew wide with fear. We continued our approach. Nobody spoke. When we were within ten feet or so, he finally spoke.

"I say, is this a stickup?"

The queen would have been proud.

THE GREAT JALPATAGUA PIG PROJECT (OR PORKY MEETS PABLO)

By Bernie Engel

Having successfully completed the Peace Corps' level-two poultry project (the one designed for city kids), my partner Steve Haas and I decided to move on to the infinitely more complex and challenging Pig Project. We figured, heck, how much harder could it be than raising chickens?

We figured wrong.

Briefly, the project involved persuading some hapless *campesino* [peasant farmer] to invest time, effort and money (his, not ours) to raise a pig under our direction (which, if you think about it for more than 10 seconds, is a ludicrous idea). We would provide the pig free of charge. This would not, however, be an ordinary pig. There were plenty of those running around Jalpatagua. No, this was to be a special baby pig bred from the finest pig parents that the grange (or 4-H or Future Farmers of America or some other farm group) had donated to Peace Corps Guatemala. The idea, I think, was to introduce the *campesino* to advanced methods of pig-raising and to improve the local pig droves. Why Steve and I, with no knowledge of even elementary pig-raising, thought we could or should do this is anyone's guess.

Being enterprising Peace Corps volunteers, we decided we should learn something about raising pigs *before* we actually got our hands on one. Peace Corps Guatemala maintained a pig-breeding facility in Rabinal, staffed by volunteers with agricultural backgrounds and training. The idea was that volunteers who decided to undertake a pig project would visit the site, which included a breeding facility, and receive training in the care and feeding of young porkers. Pig projects were so popular among volunteers that there was a waiting list for piglets. So Steve and I signed up for pig-raising 101 at Pork U (school colors, mud and you don't want to know).

The first thing we learned was that mature male pigs are known as boars and not, "Holy sh-t look at the size of those mother f—-rs!" The second thing we learned was not to get too close to the boars, especially if there was an attractive female pig, a sow, in the neighborhood. Fortunately, the boars and sows were kept in sturdy pens to prevent them from trashing the facility and perhaps eating a volunteer or two.

One of the first things we learned was how to inoculate a pig — not as straightforward as you might think (if you ever think about such things). The first thing we did was unscrew the business end of the syringe, which was the size of a turkey baster, then we crept up veeerrry carefully to a sleeping boar and jammed the needle into the beast. Then we ran like hell and hoped the pen that the local guys built was strong enough to hold the pissed off, huge pig. The boar eventually calmed down and settled back into his mud patch, when we crept up again and gently connected the rest of the syringe to the threaded end of the needle and injected the vaccine. Once this was done, we yanked out the needle and joyously celebrated survival (ours, not the pig's), complete with dancing, hugging and beer-drinking.

We were also introduced to the fine art of breeding pigs. (What follows is not for the faint of heart or those of a prudish nature).

Most people know how four-legged animals get it on. Porkers do it essentially the same way. However, we're talking about a boar that weighs half a ton and a sow that's probably worth more on the open market than I am. The point is that, left to his own devices, the boar, in the throes of porcine amour, is capable of doing serious physical damage to Mrs. (Ms.?) Sow.

To avoid catastrophe, special enclosures were built for the sows, something like packing crates, only open at one end and on top. A specially constructed ramp allowed Mr. Boar to assume the position in a manner whereby his weight shifted from the back of the sow to the sides of the box, which supported the boar. (Aren't you glad you asked?)

I don't think I have the words to describe what happened next. Let's just say the earth really did move.

By that time, Steve and I were seriously rethinking the whole pig project. Fortunately, the rest of the training didn't involve much time with the pigs. We learned about pig nutrition and breeds, how to construct a proper pen for a pig (mostly concrete floor with just enough dirt to let him root around a little to keep his snout in trim) and how to communicate with your pig — right, pig Latin! (Couldn't resist.)

We returned to Jalpatagua to begin phase two of the Pig Project Recruitment. This meant talking some poor schmuck into signing a contract with us, whereby we agreed to provide a pure-bred female pig, which he (poor schmuck) agreed to raise by our rules, but at his expense. He would have to buy cement to build the pen, and buy the medications, vaccines and feed (although CARE provided most of the feed since much of the food they brought into Guatemala for feeding programs came in spoiled.)

We also agreed that when the sow was ready to be a mother we would fix her up with a suitable partner and introduce them both to the joys of sex. When mamacita dropped her litter (that's pig talk for giving birth), poor schmuck would be required to give one female from the litter to another poor schmuck who would begin the process again. Original poor schmuck would keep all the piggies (less the one female he gave away) secure in the knowledge that he would be well on his way to becoming the Frank Perdue of Guatemala (oh wait – that's chickens).

When we finally got the guy to sign the agreement, he asked, "Where's my pig?"

"Trust us," we said.

The look on his face said, "Oh my God, I've just signed away my wife, children, house and immortal soul."

Weeks went by. Finally, the Peace Corps office lent us a jeep to drive to Rabinal to pick up our precious bundle of joy and take her back to Jalpatagua.

When we got to Rabinal, we learned that our little gal had been weaned from mom and had been on solid food for a while. I had no idea how much she weighed but she was at least the size of a small Labrador retriever. We loaded her into the back of the jeep and began the drive home.

I can't recall how long the drive took, but suffice it to say that driving a jeep down a dirt road on a steep mountainside with no guard rails while a pig tries to eat your ear is not what you'd call the joy of the open road.

Once the pig was firmly ensconced in her new quarters, chez poor schmuck *campesino*, the project fell into a predictable routine. Visit the pig, feed the pig, inoculate the pig, visit the pig, feed the pig, feed the pig, feed the pig — well you get the idea.

Eventually it came time to move on to the romantic phase of the project. We advised the experts in Rabinal that love was in the air and that our little gal (not so little at this point) was ready to become a mama among pigs. A date was set.

The Rabinal guys brought the stud boar to Jalpatagua. A number of local farmers came to see what kind of scam the lying, thieving gringos had pulled off this time. The atmosphere was something like a medieval bedding ceremony when the wedding guests accompanied the newlyweds to the bed chamber while treating them to ribald jokes and rowdy songs and poems. A good time was had by all, including Mr. and Ms. Porky, presumably.

By the time the piglets were safely delivered, our local pig owner had figured out he knew more than we did about pig-raising, which came as no surprise to me and Steve. The moment we tore up the contract — all of its provisions having been fulfilled — he told us politely to buzz off. We were more than happy to comply and soon we took off for well-deserved vacation time.

Steve may read this some day and claim none of it ever happened, and if it did, it was nothing like I've described. Well, as they say, this is my story and I'm sticking to it.

HOW MY CAT PHOEBE AND I GOT TO GUATEMALA

By Maggie Neal Kent

In the fall of 1963, I was still young, quiet, resourceful and so excited! My husband, Keni, had gone to Guatemala ahead of me. I went down on a freighter harbored in San Francisco Bay. After years with CARE in Vietnam and India without a refrigerator, we believed we needed one. So I put our refrigerator on the freighter and off I went.

On the way, we stopped at Long Beach to take on cargo. Passengers had the day off-ship. Excited and kind of "Frenchy" well dressed, I boarded a bus and told the driver I wanted to go to Los Angeles.

"Okay, but where in L.A.?"

Silence . . . then, "Anywhere in L.A. is fine."

I was raised in the South, went to a small eastern college, then to Vietnam and India. I knew nothing about L.A. The driver suggested a central downtown market with lots of food and flowers, green grass and trees.

I found no monuments, no churches, no museums, just an immense market, too big for me to want to see even one more booth. I also found a Siamese cat with kittens, and purchased one kitten along with a cat cage.

The captain at the ship's rails saw me approaching and said the cat could not come aboard; the sailors would be troubled. They considered cats on ships to be bad luck. I said I would hide the cat in the shower and the captain acquiesced. "Phoebe," a.k.a. "Sappho," would much later escape from her cage at the airport on our way home from Guatemala, but would be caught, and later accompany me to Malaysia and Costa Rica.

When the ship arrived in port on Guatemala's western coast, we pulled in as close as possible to a dirt road and jungle on the shoreline. It was rather like landing a canoe on a lake, but it was, in fact, the Pacific Ocean. The crew swung me and my cat over the water in a round basket hung by a line off a mast, dropping me on a grassy bank with trees a few feet away but no buildings in sight. I stepped out of the basket as if getting off the seat of a Ferris wheel.

A man approached me from a jeep parked at the end of the dirt road. He was Tony Durán, from CARE, who said Keni couldn't come, but he looked forward to seeing me that night.

I had a refrigerator and a suitcase full of swell maternity clothes that I had made in India where we were stationed before Guatemala. Our first child was born in India but she died in a local hospital when a storm took out the lights, including the warming bulb hanging over her. I had hepatitis and couldn't sleep with her that first night, and there were no oxygen tanks. We intended to go to CARE the next day, but, by then, she had died.

In Guatemala City, Tony brought me to a hotel where I was reunited with Keni and we all had a nice first day at the Ron Bakers'.

A few days after my arrival, President Kennedy was shot. I went to the barber shop where Keni was getting a haircut and told him the news. The world stood still in that barbershop.

Within a week of my arrival, we found a house half a block from the hotel and launched into the world of the Peace Corps. Whatever came up, I seemed to view it from 16 feet off the ground.

Somewhere down the line, in Costa Rica, I found the ground, and it is a rough trail, with surprises, pleasures, and tough maneuvers to stay on track. There are falls and plenty of recoveries. I did not do much to make things happen. I believed that if I was silent and receptive like a child, I would be drawn into the current that was best for me. I had no worries, no sense of wondering. And, something happened. I was doing!

Keni taught me the roads to towns with their odd names, the towns with one store and the small houses with little or no furniture.

I worked as a medical aide in the emergency room of the nearby general hospital about once a week. I took a six-month Red Cross course in emergency-room procedures and became part of a team with some Guatemalan *señoras de buenas familias* [women of good families] from my *barrio*. I learned hygiene, first-aid procedures and how to clean and sew *machete* or knife wounds with black thread and a needle. I especially remember the scalp wounds and extracting bullets with tweezers. We did a good job, I and the fine ladies of Guatemala City. Luckily, my Castillian Spanish was excellent because I had lived a year in Madrid.

My greatest reward in Guatemala was the birth of my son Roger. My greatest sadness was leaving. In a flash, we were gone! Our last Peace Corps party. Keni and I were instructed to move to Malaysia, and I think we left the refrigerator behind.

Late in life, I lost the open, quiet-mindedness of my youth and learned to suffer, but also to give and take good things to make up for the difficulties.

My son, Roger, is a wonderful person. Eliza, my daughter born in Malaysia, often lives and researches books alone in remote villages. I am grandmother now to Eliza's adopted Guatemalan boy, Philip Rodrigo Kent. With eyes as black as licorice, eyes that hold onto you, he smiles so big I fall into his face.

I look forward to Guatemala III's large or small reunions. It is good to put a special mark on ourselves and our group from time to time. Our laughter and friendship is powerful.

MEANWHILE, BACK IN NEW YORK ... ETC.

By Carolyn Plage

Meanwhile, back in New York, one Guatemala III Peace Corps volunteer waited impatiently for healing after surgery on a pilonital cyst at the bottom of her spine. The healing was slow, including a setback requiring a second surgery. Time weighed heavily with games of solitaire, readings of James Bond novels, pillow case and dresser scarf embroidery. The mailman now and then brought words of encouragement or inspiration from those already settled at their sites in Guatemala. Perhaps the only good thing about this wait was the chance to visit the World's Fair in New York City twice. Finally in June, the doctor and the bosses in Washington, DC agreed that I could leave for Guatemala, but would have "limited" duty, which meant being stationed in Guatemala City near good medical facilities.

So in June, 1964, I arrived in Guatemala City, stayed in the Palace Hotel a few days, and then was taken to Zone 5 and the family I lived with for the next four months. It was a busy household with a storefront selling groceries, *tamales* and such, all made by *la señora* and her hired help. I had a room, a bed and a dresser to myself next to the bathroom, and a shower with cold water only. I remember my surprise when I learned that the four girls in the family (ages 9 to 21) all slept in the same bed — maybe a double bed but no larger. I don't think I ever understood where the youngest boy, age 8, and his two college-age brothers slept. With so many people in the house and just a small dining table, there were shifts for meals and I generally was on the late shift. I therefore ate with the two older boys, one enrolled in the military academy and the other at the university. They knew very little English, but wanted to talk about so much. I found myself trying to answer questions about U.S. race problems, communism vs. capitalism, and more. I often went to bed with a headache from searching so hard for answers and putting them in Spanish, trying to provide answers to questions difficult even in English.

There were chickens running around the inner courtyard, flies everywhere, and always people coming and going. But, it was peaceful commotion until the return of Papa — fired from his job up north where he'd been supervising workers on some *finca* [landed estate]. It soon became apparent why he'd been fired, as his fondness for "*aguardiente*" [liquor] proved to be uncontrollable, and so was he.

My assignment in a nearby *colonia* was not very clear. The school already had a milk distribution program. Somehow I wound up organizing a young boys' basketball team — the Jets — and a cooking group with a half dozen girls. We made banana bread with *incaparina* (a powdered substance of wheat, corn meal and added proteins, all lacking in the Guatemalan diet). I'm sure they never used the recipe again, but all said the bread was "delicious." I met with the Tropical Boys' Club — so it says in notes I have found — but I can't remember anything in particular that we dealt with. Supposedly their purpose was the betterment of their community. I became close friends with one particular family. We cooked in Doña's [Spanish title for married women or widows] dirt-floor kitchen. I remember it was another instance of a strong-willed, hard-working woman with a man whose work was located someplace else, and when he came home, his drunkenness distressed the entire household.

There were several basketball games on the dirt courts outside the school with my Jets sometimes participating. Two particular incidents have stuck in my mind. Once during a game there came a downpour such as everyone expected each afternoon in the rainy season. Many onlookers, myself included, sought shelter under the eaves of the building. As we stood there, a few of us were suddenly being bitten by fire ants that rushed out of the anthill we'd apparently disturbed. At another game, the *gringita* was pelted with several small stones. I wasn't hurt, but my friends from the *colonia* were very concerned. It was speculated that the thrower had been a *comunista* from the *barrancas* below. Although the *colonia*, Chacra Saravia, was populated with poor folks living in small quarters with dirt floors, outhouses, and no luxuries, the people who lived in the *barrancas* were even worse off. Their houses were makeshift creations that would often fall down during severe rains. There was no electricity or running water. The people of the *barrancas* were viewed as the lowest of low life. I learned this when a bright-eyed, good-looking, curly-haired boy in a too-small green polo shirt wanted to join the Jets. The boys already on the team objected because Carlos lived in the *barranca*. Somehow I persuaded them to let Carlos join our team and he proved to be a good player. He always wore that same green shirt, perhaps the only one he owned.

Back home in *la tienda,* at least until Papa came on the scene, life was good. Weekends I was invited to go with the family and neighbors to attend *repasos* [reviews] in the neighborhood, dancing the *cumbia* to live *marimba* bands, and drinking *aguardiente* and/or thick black coffee. I loved the music (still do) and the dancing and somehow survived *los triagitos* [the little sips]. I quickly learned the one way to be polite but refuse a drink was to say, "*No, me hace daño.*"["It doesn't agree with me."] Anyone hearing those words seemed to assume that you refused the drink because of an ulcer or other intestinal problem. In my case, as I recall, there were a few bouts with amebic dysentery, something that impacted many a Peace Corps volunteer.

When Papa came back home, my privacy in the household was threatened. The atmosphere became tense and grim. I presented my problem to the Peace Corps office and we arrived at the decision that I should move into an apartment in Zone 1. With guidance from Joe Sklar [a Peace Corps assistant], I then set out to investigate other possible avenues for future Peace Corps projects in the city. I settled on working at the *Biblioteca Infantil* [Children's Library] off the plaza in *Parque Colon* [Columbus Park]. I became the librarian's assistant and set up a variety of programs — movies and crafts to encourage the children of the area to use the library. Most of my time was spent teaching English to three different age groups. The oldest group was comprised of a few university students and others close to my own age. We took trips together — picnics and hikes and shared some joyful times. Some of the library visitors were the city's shoeshine boys. With my guitar in hand, I'd lead the children in singing songs, some in Spanish, some in English. I always wondered what real good I was doing for the Guatemalans, but eventually concluded that, if nothing else, I helped the people I met know "for real" a *gringa* who didn't speak too loud, wear bright-colored shirts, have money to burn, and carry a camera.

I'll never forget the day I arrived at the library and my boss could tell I was upset about something. She pried until, with a few tears in my eyes, I told her the reasons for my sorrow. Her first comment was that she did not know that *gringos* cried. The Guatemalans also saw that we Peace Corps volunteers were not dressed in the latest high fashions. It seems like I lived in that poor grey wrap-around skirt!

A vacation in Mexico was a highlight of the year. (How many days of vacation did we get?) My visit to Mexico City and Acapulco with Nola had me convinced that I should return to study at the University of Mexico after my Peace Corps service. Nola and I traveled by Rutas Lima to Guatemala's northern border in a little beat-up green bus with chickens and people inside and on top. At the Mexican border we boarded a much larger Greyhound-type bus to Mexico City. My fondest memories are of the then recently- opened anthropology museum. It was awesome! The murals by Diego Rivera and others also impressed me greatly. At the university, while we were doing the tourist thing and taking pictures, two male students offered to take our photo in front of a mural and then invited us out. I don't remember if we went. (Hey Nola, are you there?)

In Acapulco, I loved the beach and once again, two friendly Mexicans charmed we *gringas* into joining them on their boat for a swim in the bay. We dove for oysters and ate them aboard the boat — raw with a bit of hot sauce — and drank milk from coconuts. We also got to snorkel, something I'd never done before. When I was peering underwater and seeing wonderfully colored fish, I tried to yell out my delight and wound up sputtering and choking on the salty seawater. Another first was eating octopus for dinner at some restaurant in Acapulco.

I did return to Mexico for a second vacation with Marge Bradbury, the Guatemala III volunteer in her sixties, but never went to grad school there. Instead, I returned to New Mexico and attended grad school at the University in Albuquerque and lived and worked there from 1967 to 1970. I have continued to indulge my passion for Mexican culture by frequenting restaurants serving Mexican cuisine and enjoying my collection of CDs and tapes of Javier Solis and other more recent Mexican singers and musicians.

A SPEECH TO HAWTHORNE REFORMED CHURCH'S WOMEN'S CLUB — FEBRUARY, 1964

By Carolyn Plage

Some of you are already aware that there was an error on the cards you received about this meeting. As it read, I am supposed to talk about my experiences in Guatemala with the Peace Corps. I'd love to do just that but I haven't been there yet. I was in training at New Mexico State University from Sept. 19 to Dec. 14 and have been delayed at home for medical reasons up to now. I hope to be able to join my fellow volunteers soon.

Our group began with 69 trainees; eight were "selected-out," or as we so fondly said, were "given the axe" for medical reasons or because the "head shrinkers" didn't think they had what it would take to make good Peace Corps volunteers. Two resigned, one only four weeks after we began, and the other, the last week, to marry a brother of one of our Spanish-speaking instructors. Thus, there are presently 59 volunteers in our Guatemala III program. The Guatemala I and II groups have been down there for a few months participating in a program under the National Agricultural Extension Service. About 26 volunteers with farm backgrounds are helping organize 4-H clubs and assisting Guatemalan extension service agents in improving agriculture and home-making practices. Another 50 volunteers are working with the National Indian Service in the western area of the country.

Our project is entitled "Community Development" and we are to help administer a school lunch program set up by CARE. There are 40 volunteers scattered about in small villages in the central and eastern highlands in groups of threes, usually one fellow and two gals. Besides these, there are about 12 members in Guatemala City, the capital of the country. They are stationed in the poorer areas of the city.

The school lunch includes milk and the aforementioned *incaparina*. The volunteers, with the help of local mothers, whenever they can be recruited, prepare the lunch and distribute it.

The CARE/Peace Corps program has been set up to encourage general community development, with the school program designed to function as an entrée into the community and as a stepping-stone for further projects. There are many possibilities for efforts beyond the lunches, such as building recreation facilities, forming local sports teams, planting a school garden, beginning a town library, or initiating manual arts classes. Health and sanitation could be substantially improved with such basic things as garbage disposal, building latrines, encouraging the people to take preventive measures to fight illnesses, and offering nutrition and literacy classes for both children and adults in their own language and in English.

As in all Peace Corps projects, the volunteer is to encourage the people to experiment for themselves and to utilize on their own, the human, financial, and technical resources that their country affords.

My friends writing to me from Guatemala have not been specific about what has happened in the month gone by, but then perhaps not much has occurred in so short a time. The first one and a half weeks were spent in an orientation program and in receiving their assignments. There have been three of us delayed in the States and we have exchanged news as we receive it. So far, at least two volunteers have gotten so sick they had to go back to the capital city for hospitalization. Perhaps they were victims of dysentery or the milder illness that we call "green chili trots." Some are finding their conversing ability limiting. We had four hours of Spanish classes daily while in training, but for those who had never studied the language in high school or college the going isn't easy. After the volunteers were given their assignments, they had to look for housing. In some villages the local officials had already arranged living quarters for their Peace Corps volunteers.

Nola Alberts was stationed in the village of Mataquescuintla in the highlands, with Marcia Lang and Bryce Hamilton. The people there are *Ladinos* [non-Indians], who speak Spanish — as opposed to the indigenous people, who speak various Indian dialects. Nola wrote, "Our town is just great. They had a reception waiting for us when we arrived, complete with speeches, *marimba* band, flowers, and dancing. We were just stunned! Then they showed us our house. It rents for $25 but it is huge with eight rooms. The people in Mataquescuintla are really wonderful. They have done so much for us already and are really fired up and enthusiastic. I just hope it keeps up. So far we only have a table, two beds, three mattresses, and a dresser for the eight rooms. But we've already had visitors and brewed them a pot of coffee on our kerosene stove and they didn't mind sitting on the beds."

Another letter from Nola had this to say: "Marcia and I are both kind of punchy tonight as practically everything we did went wrong today. You know, just one of those days. At least we could laugh everything off. She's going to be starting knitting classes a couple of days a week and I plan to start practicing with the girls' basketball team here in town. There are some really great girls on the team and some very good players. I'm eager to get to know them all better."

A letter from Tim Kraft, stationed in El Petén with Carol Bellamy, states, "It is good to be here, and I think this is one of the better assignments. We've stepped right into the middle of a high-powered organization and it has helped a lot. It's called FYDEP, a special semi-military government agency that has been very good to us. We're staying in their camp, right on the lake, until the house they obtained and paid for is ready. As this assignment is going to be fairly mobile, involving schools in six to eight towns, they've also put a jeep at our disposal. As I see it now, the job will be mostly with the schools and possibly a preschool milk program for kids one to five, and English classes. The Petén environment was pretty badly distorted in the reports we heard. We're having winter now (August to February) and today was hot and sunny. Flores, being in the center of Petén and on a lake, has a varying climate. The flies aren't bad and I haven't seen a mosquito yet."

Some volunteers have running water in their houses, as in the city, but the water is never hot. Most of it has to be boiled to kill the possible germs. When there *is* electricity, it is not in operation all day. In Nola's village, lights go out at 10:00 p.m. and she says, "It's a good thing the lights go out then or we would have visitors all night long."

Jay Jackson, stationed in one of the poorer areas of the city, is living with two other Peace Corps volunteers. He wrote, "We are living in a five-room place with flush toilet, running water, cold shower, and a woman who cooks, washes, irons, and does a little cleaning for $12 a month. All of us in the city have a refrigerator."

Perhaps it is a bit too soon to say the Peace Corps is a success in the politically hot country of Guatemala, but in certain respects we are optimistic that some good will come of our being there. The Peace Corps volunteers are gaining experience in seeing another country and another people, and the Guatemalans are becoming acquainted with a new kind of North American — one who isn't a businessman, or government official, or tourist, one who certainly doesn't have a lot of money to toss around, and one who is happy to sit at his or her table and share rice and beans. The Guatemalans and volunteers are working together and friendships will undoubtedly be made as each participates in community activities.

Back in El Petén, Tim has already begun to share experiences with the Guatemalans. And he seems to be having a swell time doing so. He wrote that he broke the ice with the head of FYDEP after winning $7 in his poker game, and he danced and drank at their *fiesta*, swam at the beach of a nearby island, had a few chess games and acquired another friend who will loan his speedboat whenever he wants it.

I haven't been to Guatemala yet, but I certainly enjoyed the training since Sept 19, from our mountain-climbing expeditions to the 10-hour classes each day. I played much volleyball and basketball, chopped off a chicken's head, de-feathered and cut up the poor thing, and attended lectures on American history, Guatemalan culture, and Communism and Democracy.

We spent two weeks "south of the border down Mexico way." That field trip came about halfway through our training. We were in the state of

Chihuahua. Our only help came from Spanish-speaking Mexican students who went along with each group. Our "guides" to Madera knew about as little of the town as we did, but were wonderful friends. One handsome young man taught me how to sing some Mexican *rancheros* and accompany the songs on my guitar. Madera was a town of 8,000, about the same population as Hawthorne, N.Y., my home town. But, with Madera's pigs and cows and burros wandering about on the dirt road through the middle of town, it was not quite the same. In our two weeks there, we could initiate no projects as we hope to do in Guatemala, but we spent our days speaking Spanish and learning about the town and its people and making many friends. The experience gave us a feeling of what it is like to live a life in another country quite different from what we've already known. As for me, I loved every minute in Chihuahua, Mexico, and am looking forward to beginning work in Guatemala.

THE QUESTION OF PETS

By Marcia K. Lang

The premier girls' basketball match between Mataquescuintla and Panajachel had finally arrived. Before traveling to it, I made arrangements for my menagerie. I left my dog, Xocomil, with Priscilla [Takano]. Pepe, my spider monkey, boarded at the Henshaws, a family from the University of Chicago who lived down the road. Their three small children were excited to care for him.

It was a unique trip: competitive matches between Peace Corps sites. Eight members of the Panajachel basketball team and their coach, Aurora, were excited about traveling to unknown areas where stiff competition loomed on the horizon. They also looked forward to the social activities planned in their honor. We embarked on our travels at the break of dawn as hues of luminescent rose petals tiptoed across the horizon. Lucinda, the captain, flagged down "El Rapido," the express bus to the capital where we transferred at the main terminal to Don Pancho's bus for Jalapa. Pancho's son, Osmin, played on the basketball team, and Nola [Alberts], my roommate, asked him to save us front-row seats.

Arriving at our final destination, the girls became acquainted with their hosts. Later all of the players gathered on the new basketball court for a friendly practice. All of the team members appeared a bit cocky and over-confident, yet if you peeled back the thin layer of bravado, you'd see them trembling like the hoop's taut wire rim.

Our first game was scheduled for 10 a.m. Everyone appeared on the court two hours early for warm-ups. I commandeered a pivotal position on the bleachers erected especially for the games and watched Aurora put our team through warm-up drills.

Shortly after the game started, Paco, the nervous, wizened clerk from the telegraph office tapped me on the shoulder: "Miss Marcia, a very important message is waiting for you."

"Oh, Paco, please don't bother me. I'm watching the game."

"No, seño, it's urgent, come with me."

"Ok, ok, I'll come with you, but let's just watch the finish of this quarter." The teams were well-matched; I didn't want to miss a second. When the quarter ended Paco hustled me to the telegraph office where Don Meme greeted me with a rather puzzled look. "¿Quien es Pepe?"[Who is Pepe?"].

"Pepe? Pepe is my pet monkey." As Don Meme nodded his head, I noticed a palpable sadness in his eyes. He thrust a telegram into my hands.

"Marcia, this is NO JOKE – Pepe died frothing at the mouth! Sending his head to Ministry of Health for examinations. Pepe bit the Henshaws' two little children. Your friend, Priscilla."

I lowered myself onto a bench. What happened to poor little Pepe? Was he rabid? George and I had taken precautions to inoculate both monkeys before we left Ecuador! My head reeled. The Henshaw children would need rabies shots. Priscilla didn't know that Pepe had bitten me in Ecuador. Those little bites seemed so harmless. Pepe's tiny razor-like teeth had merely drawn a few drops of bright blood! I grew queasy and nauseous.

Meme asked, "Why are you so upset, Marcia?"

"Oh Meme, what a dreadful mess and it's all my fault. On vacation in Ecuador I picked up a cute little monkey that seemed so harmless. I wasn't thinking, was I? Now, I'm terrified that he died of rabies — 'frothing at the mouth,' for heaven's sake! Oh, I never should have gotten him. You know, we're not supposed to have pets, certainly not monkeys. And the Henshaws must be worried sick about their children."

I couldn't stop blabbering. "One of my best friends, Mike [Schwartz], who lives in the Petén, had a dog that got rabies . . . also frothing at the mouth . . . and they had to send him to New Orleans for shots. Oh Meme, what am I going to do?"

Mentally I composed a telegram to good old "Doctor Nick," our infamous Peace Corps doctor, as I wandered back to the bleachers. I don't even remember who won the first game.

Nola caught wind of the commotion. When time permitted she ran over. "Marcia, what's the ruckus about?"

When I told her, she said, "Oh, *puchikas*, that's awful. I can just hear Nick now. He'll be furious — lose it for sure. Remember his stellar performance during your helicopter rescue?"

"What'll I do? I'm scared he will have me terminated!"

It was only Saturday morning. There were two more games to be played, and a dance had been planned for that evening. Sunday was scheduled as our travel day.

Noticing our huddle, Aurora bounced over. "What's going on?"

I brought her up to speed. We all agreed to leave the travel plans intact. I would stop in Guatemala City and Aurora would continue to Panajachel with the basketball team.

It wasn't long before everyone heard about the problem. This was big news, entertainment for the town folk, but everyone appreciated the gravity of the situation. Rabies was a well known, much-feared disease.

The series of 14 rabies shots would be required because the waiting period had reached the maximum time limit. I composed a telegram to Nick. *"Bitten by monkey. Need rabies shot. Arriving Sunday, Sept. 28, your office at 13:00. Marcia Lang"*

Priscilla got my next telegram. *"Stopping in city to start rabies shots. Ask health center to hold sufficient vaccine for Henshaw children and me. Returning late Monday. Marcia"*

I thought the children had time to wait for the test results, which took about two weeks. However, their parents would undoubtedly opt to start their shots immediately.

The moment I crossed the threshold of Nick's office he started. "How could you? How could you be so blindly irresponsible? AND STUPID?"

I was unable to utter a word, terrified, not of Nick, but of the ravages of the disease.

"Where did you get that damn monkey? It was yours, wasn't it?" he hissed.

"Yes, Nick, he was mine. I'm sorry Nick, I really am."

I couldn't stomach telling him the truth, that I'd smuggled Pepe from Ecuador. He probably didn't realize I had been traveling out of country. I was in enough hot water and didn't want to aggravate the situation. We both knew he had little control over volunteers and their pets. Pacing the office, he grabbed a vial from the refrigerator and commanded, "Get ready!"

I steeled myself, determined not to flinch or cry. "This needle goes into your stomach, so pull your shirt out and. . ." It was the largest needle I'd ever seen. He swabbed me with alcohol, then plunged the needle into the soft folds of my stomach.

"You'll need another 13 shots." He thrust a styrofoam box loaded with ice and vials of vaccine into my hands. "Make sure the ice doesn't melt! Keep the vaccine refrigerated. They do have a refrigerator at the health center in Panajachel, don't they?" he boomed.

"Yes, Nick, they do." I whimpered.

In his best bedside manner he screamed, "Now, get out of my sight! AND FOR GOD'S SAKE, DON'T PICK UP ANY MORE DISEASED ANIMALS!"

"Yes, sir!"

Trembling, I bolted from the office. I knew I was wrong and had feared not only a dreadful interrogation about Pepe but also that Nick might find out about my dog Xocomil. Worried about the erratic electrical supply in the village, I offered fervent silent prayers that the electricity in Panajachel wouldn't fail in the next few weeks and that Nick wouldn't find out about my dog.

I hailed a cab for Zone 7 and spent the night with the Peace Corps guys there before heading back. I craved the company of sympathetic friends ... and a cold beer, even though alcohol should probably not have been consumed in combination with the rabies drug.

Fortunately, the health center had a stock of rabies vaccine for the children. The shots were incredibly painful. The huge needle was blunt and the liquid stung as it traveled through my stomach in search of its target. Humongous red welts erupted on my stomach and itched incessantly. I wondered how I could discreetly scratch the inflamed welts and I dreaded the remaining injections. Nothing relieved the discomfort except the news from the ministry of health that Pepe was not rabid!

A soft faded white bump remains on my right forearm from the rabies shots we received during training in Las Cruces. There are no bumps on my stomach from the 14 shots. They're embedded in the soft white folds of my brain.

SPINNING WEBS

By Marcia K. Lang

Spiders silently spun their webs. The tendrils swam seductively through the air in slow-motion, trying to escape.

I heard his voice: *What the hell do you want to go to Guatemala for? It's so primitive! You know, don't you, that you could die there?* My father's prophecy was coming true. In an odd sort of way, I felt comforted hearing his voice.

"Dad, Dad, how will I ever get out of this alive?"

I was paralyzed. Numbness crept stealthily on silent spindly legs, up and through my body, stopping for rest in the middle of my icy nose. I couldn't taste anything. Miraculously I could still see, hear and swallow, but I couldn't talk.

My father had envisioned my death in the hinterlands of Guatemala. I pondered his fears as the hours slowly ticked by. The locals seemed to agree with him. Women, men and children came to pay their last respects. Carrying lit candles in their left hands, they prayed constantly, while crossing themselves with their right. Humble folk, they genuflected at my bedside and touched me or the bed to demonstrate their concern.

The previous day, Nola, my roommate, and I had arrived in Sampaquisoy from our base in Mataquescuintla. It was to be a three-day work trip. We were the guests of honor at the evening dance. Shortly after the music started I excused myself to find the outhouse. Something wasn't agreeing with me.

My stomach knotted in excruciating cramps. I was thankful I made it in time to the latrine.

Woozy, I returned to the dance and asked for another Coca-Cola, hoping it would calm my stomach. In a half-hour I excused myself again; the time between my disappearances was getting shorter.

"Nola," I whispered, "I'm leaving. I feel awful."

Back in our room, I crawled on top of the bed and shivered uncontrollably, then dozed off. Jolted by cramps, I crept inside my sleeping bag and pulled a green woolen-blanket over the top, hoping it would take away the chill, but I got colder and colder.

"*¿Vos, como te va?*" I heard Nola say as she entered the room, inquiring about me.

"I feel dreadful . . . can't think straight . . . I'm freezing. . . ."

When dances were held in our honor it was expected that we would dance with almost everyone. Nola light-heartedly complained about having to dance with each man at least twice since I wasn't there. She was a good sport. I figured she could handle it.

The latrine was an American-sized city block from the main house, buzzing with horrible black flies. I couldn't stomach it and didn't know how I'd conceal my soiled clothes or return unnoticed to the bedroom. I threw up in the bushes. Thank God it was dark!

Clutching my flashlight and a roll of toilet paper, I stumbled back to the room. I found a warm sweater and clean jeans and put a basin next to my head before lying down. The vomiting wouldn't stop.

Poor Nola had to bury my vomit and wastes in between the coffee bushes so they wouldn't contaminate anything.

My body underwent a slow metamorphosis. Within an hour, numbness slowly crept through it, inch by inch, until both legs were paralyzed.

Nola returned. I begged for liquids. She eyed me like I was hallucinating. Only a few minutes before I had refused liquids.

I pointed to my toes and whispered, "My toes, they're numb. I can't move them. I can't move my legs either!"

She started for the door, saying, "Don't move, I'll be back in a jiff. I'm going to tell our host and Beto."

A dark green Coleman lantern glowed on a table near the door casting eerie reflections on the rafters. I followed the night inhabitants as they crawled, slowly exploring their territory. They took on larger than life proportions. I was certain a tarantula hovered over me, poised to drop.

I could hear worried conversation outside the room. Nola seemed to stride in and out of the room nonstop, while I dozed on and off.

Dawn's light finally splintered through the window. Nola joined Beto in the courtyard as he prepared his horse. He was going for help, a five-hour ride down the mountain to Colis.

Like the spiders I thought I'd seen, everyone began spinning a web. Immediate neighbors checked on me so Nola could rest. Beto galloped down the mountainside, arriving in Mataquescuintla in a record four hours. He went directly to our house and asked for Don Bryce.

They ran to the telegraph office to find Don Meme. Bryce wrote: "Marcia paralyzed in village of Sampaquisoy. Don't know details. Send help immediately. Please respond. Bryce Hamilton." Meme sent it to the CARE office.

Keni Kent was about to leave the CARE office when he received the telegram several hours later. Luckily, Doctor Nick was still there.

Keni's reply: "Help is on the way. I will fly to Sampaquisoy by helicopter. Doctor Nick will drive to Mataquescuintla in his jeep. Prepare horse and guides for him. Stay calm. Keni."

All the ~~Peace Corp~~s people in Mataquescuintla had learned about the unfolding drama. The reactions were astounding. Many assumed I had fallen off my horse, suffered a spinal injury and was paralyzed.

Bryce packed his duffel bag and looked up as the last rays of sunlight shone on the giant spider weaving his web. Trapping an unsuspecting bug in his net, he silently spun the silken threads round and round so it couldn't escape.

A RESCUE IN THE MOUNTAINS

By Marcia K. Lang

Keni Kent left his home in Guatemala City at 4 a.m. to reach El Progresso at dawn. A helicopter and pilot would be waiting for him. On meeting the pilot he remembered giving Dr. Nick his only detailed map. The pilot only had a simple map of the region that pinpointed the capital city and the departments of each Central American country.

Keni had studied a detailed map in his office with Nick and hoped he could remember the layout of the terrain. But the mountainous range turned into an incomprehensible puzzle. He followed the forks in the river. When he thought they had flown long enough, they decided to land. The pilot sighted a soccer field that looked promising.

Unbeknownst to them, the villagers in this region harbored a deep fear of cannibalism. From infancy, they had listened to tales about "foreign devils" who would descend on their village, steal their children, fatten them up and eat them.

As the terrifying helicopter circled above the village, parents gathered their children and hid them from sight, under beds, behind stacked crops in the fields, and in the shadows. The parents also feared for themselves, so the mothers hid as well.

Descending from the bright blue sky, the helicopter appeared like an evil spider. It thrashed over the fields, searching for a safe landing place, then touched ground. A wary group of men surrounded the helicopter, armed with machetes, prepared to defend their families.

Delighted at the smooth landing, Keni emerged and, unaware of the fear, flashed his winning smile and asked: "Ola, señores, have we landed in Sampaquisoy?"

"Sampaquisoy?" they all repeated warily, looking from one to the other.

Not sure if the men had understood, Keni repeated the name of the village, a little louder and a little slower. "SAM – PA – QUI – SOY. Have we arrived?"

Relieved, patting their machetes, the men told them they were in the wrong village and gave them curt directions.

Meanwhile, I lay inert in Sampaquisoy, staring at the ceiling in my sick room, watching the spiders spin webs. I heard a commotion in the courtyard. Nola burst into the room, shouting, "Help is on the way.

Beto is back. He, Bryce and Don Meme sent a telegram to CARE asking for help."

Far below us, Bryce, Dr. Nick and Santiago plodded up the mountainside, while Keni and the pilot circled the mountainous terrain looking for another soccer field.

I later learned that Nick muttered throughout his journey: "How much do you want to bet that she's dead when we get there?" Bryce prayed he was wrong.

Word spread through the village that help was on the way. Every mother who passed by made the sign of the cross over me, prayed and then humbly beseeched: "Miss Marcia, do you think the doctor could see my sick child when he gets here? My parents? My brother?" Everyone had an urgent request. I just blinked my eyes in agreement.

No health workers, let alone doctors, had ever visited this village. This was historic. Maybe something good would come of this after all, I hoped.

The villagers in Sampaquisoy also harbored fears of cannibalism. Beto advised everyone that help was on the way, but we never dreamed a helicopter would be arriving to rescue me.

Two days later, as mysteriously as the paralysis had arrived, it slowly left my body, inch by inch, limb by limb, silently slipping away, just as it had mysteriously crept in.

"Nola, I can talk!" We rejoiced in the miracle.

Keni landed in another strange village, where more inhabitants hid their children from sight. Bryce and Nick continued to trudge up the mountain.

Pale, feverish and limp, I was sopping wet. My jeans were soiled, my sleeping bag soaked. Nola loaned me her only piece of clean, dry clothing, an outlandish black flowered muumuu. What a sight! But it covered me in warmth and dryness. I didn't care. I was grateful to be standing, walking and speaking.

The diarrhea returned so I rested in bed. The village women followed our instructions for boiling my drinking water. Nola brought me a pitcher of warm Tang. It was safe to drink but so yucky. I never thought I'd hate our staple liquid. My thirst was insatiable.

Late in the morning, I heard the people shouting wildly. I staggered into the sunlight toward the noise. A helicopter circled overhead, stirring up dust, searching for a safe landing place. Villagers ducked for cover. The spidery creature landed in a vacant field.

The door opened and Nola and Keni hugged, thumping each other on the back. "Holy cow," I shouted, "it's Keni! How on earth did he ever find this place?"

I stumbled toward the hillside. In seconds he was hugging me. "Marcia, thank God you're alive," he shouted. "*Puchicas!* Am I ever glad to see you!"

Tears rolled down my cheeks as Nola filled him in. It wasn't just me. Nola, our hosts, the villagers, the students, teachers: everyone was part of the ordeal, she explained. I was relieved to be with Keni and to learn that help had always been on the way.

"Look kiddo, you need rest. Stay in bed. Nick and Bryce will be arriving in a few hours. You'll fly to the city with Nick and check into the hospital. I'll go back to your site with Bryce and Nola." Keni walked me back to the *rancho* then went with Nola to meet with the village parents. "I want to hear firsthand about their concerns," he said.

I told him that as I lay paralyzed in bed for two days the villagers prayed over me — and when they heard Dr. Nick was coming they begged to bring their sick children to him. "Keni, he has to see them," I said.

"Wonderful, Marcia, Nick will love it." Keni said.

I slept deeply and suddenly Bryce and Nick were knocking on the door. Nick pushed Bryce aside and strode to my bedside. "Who in the hell do you think you are, dragging me all the way up this mountainside for nothing?" He pounded on my bedside with his fist. "What a waste of my time," he sputtered.

Bryce was dumbstruck.

"Nick," I said, "I lay in this bed for two days, totally paralyzed, wondering if I'd ever get out of here . . ."

He started to interrupt.

"No Nick. It's my turn. You listen to me. I was paralyzed for two days, with a raging fever that still hasn't subsided. I'm plagued with vomiting and diarrhea. I don't know what it is or was. But as I lay here paralyzed, the villagers passed by my bed, blessed me, prayed for me . . . don't interrupt me!" I pointed at him with a trembling finger.

"When they heard help was on the way, Nick, meaning YOU, a doctor, the mothers returned. As they prayed for me, they asked if the doctor could see their sick child or parent. You know what? Even though I couldn't talk, I promised them, with a slight blink of my eyes, that you would attend to all of them."

The redness started to leave his face. His rage softened.

"Nick, take your little black bag into the courtyard. The people are lined up, waiting for you. For two days they've prayed for your help. Go to them!"

I prayed that his meager supply of medicines would hold out for the long line.

Bryce came over to the bed and hugged me. "Marcia, I'm so glad you're alive."

"Did you really think I was dead?"

"Well, in a way. Beto left without giving me much information other than the fact you were paralyzed. Then Nick came and during the whole ride he kept muttering: 'How much do you want to bet she's dead when we get there!' I don't know where that idea came from!"

When it was time to leave, Bryce and Keni made a chair with their arms linked together and carried me, clad in Nola's wild muumuu, to the helicopter.

I flew back with Nick. We didn't say one word to each other. I sat in front next to the pilot. He knew the way back, so we arrived in Guatemala City in less than 45 minutes. Nick took me to the hospital, checked me in and said he'd return the next day. I didn't care if I ever saw him again.

What a relief to bathe, then slide between cool, clean sheets. Nurses and attendants poked and prodded. They took so many vials of blood I thought I'd need a transfusion. In the evening an unknown doctor, dressed in his whites, stopped by my bedside. "Well, did they find the amoebas?" he asked, chalking it up as mere dysentery.

Dear God, I thought, Nick did it again. I'm in the loony bin!

"I don't know, doctor, isn't that supposed to be your job?"

I wanted to go home to Colis. I felt fine, just weak. I don't remember seeing Nick again at the hospital. He probably sent that other nut case doctor in his place. I stayed in the hospital a few days for a series of inconclusive tests. The staff had never heard of an amoeba that causes paralysis. No one knew anything.

Many Peace Corps colleagues came to visit. Doug Taber and Dave Siebert used to hang out with me in training and we loved to drink cold beers at the Billy the Kid Bar & Grill. They offered to sneak in a six pack. When I declined, they knew I wasn't well.

After being discharged, I spent a night with Keni and his wife, Neal, in the comfort of their gracious home in Zone 10. They lavished me with tender love and care. I thought about my parents and how grateful they would have been to know them. Keni typed his detailed report, justifying the need for a helicopter rescue. We rehashed the details.

How thankful I was that my father's predictions hadn't come true. I didn't die in the mountains, but it was a close call.

When I got back to Colis, it tickled me when I was given a nickname: *La Dama Araña* — Spiderwoman! The helicopter reminded them of the spiders that dangled from the rafters.

PEACE CORPS MEMORIES

By Dave Smits

I'm convinced that my Peace Corps service altered my perspectives on the things that really matter in life and was critical in shaping my values. But that's far too vague a generalization! Besides, I'm too much of an iconoclast to want to give the impression that everything about the experience was mint juleps and honeysuckle. The most striking thing about Peace Corps volunteers of my vintage was our unrealistic expectation that we could better the world before lunch time. Our conception of a better world was based on the one with which we were familiar. I hoped to remake at least the part of the world where I would serve in my nation's image — a presumptuous goal at best. Furthermore, the vast majority of us were too young and green to bring to the job the farsightedness and street smarts essential to doing it well. In truth, most of us were immature, self-important, culturally arrogant, and utterly blind to our own failings. In other words, our noble experiment was conducted by flawed human beings.

But if it is true that we had our share of human failings, it is also true, I think, that most of us may have been at our very best at that tender stage of our lives. We wanted what was best for our fellow human beings and we were willing to make personal sacrifices, take risks, endure adversity, and work tirelessly to make the world a better place. At the conclusion of our service, few of us felt we had accomplished much, although we had made enduring friendships and touched some lives directly. But the world is a better place with Peace Corps "types" in it. I'm proud to have been a part of an organization whose members tried to do more with their lives than just "make money" or "have fun."

I had the good fortune to share my Peace Corps experience with my life-partner, my dear wife, Pat. We have been married since Hector was a pup, and I've often said to her that our marriage has endured because we both have short memories and because of our Peace Corps service together. Every inconvenience, challenge, and disappointment we have endured since then has been a piece of cake compared to what we handled in Guatemala and, more importantly, compared to the struggles of the Guatemalans themselves. The challenges that we confronted in our service in Guatemala were made more fixable and less daunting because of the assistance and the example of our fellow-volunteers, who provided practical solutions and inspiration or just sounding boards for our ideas and grumblings. Our Peace Corps service got our marriage off on the right foot. Also, the bonds we formed with other volunteers became one of our most cherished life-blessings.

For Pat and me, the most distinctive feature of our Peace Corps service was being the first married couple, to our knowledge, to have a child born while on duty. Certainly, we were the first in Guatemala. Pat became pregnant while we were training in Las Cruces, New Mexico. Her pregnancy was confirmed when we returned to Wisconsin for Christmas, just after our training. We decided to keep the news to ourselves, fearing that if we told Peace Corps officials, they would not allow us to go to Guatemala.

When we learned that we would be assigned to a remote village, we realized that we had no choice but to tell the CARE officials, under whom we would be working in Guatemala, that Pat was pregnant. To our delight, they agreed to keep our secret but decided that Pat must live close to Guatemala City to obtain good medical care. We were overjoyed by their cooperation. Apparently, there was no official policy on pregnancy when we joined the Peace Corps. When we finally told the director, a few months before Susie was born, he granted us permission to stay, provided that Pat could continue working and that we would assume all expenses.

Ironically, as it turned out, our baby was our greatest asset as Peace Corps volunteers. Just like Sacagawea, the Shoshoni woman who carried her baby while accompanying the Lewis and Clark expedition, and whose baby convinced the Native Americans encountered en route that the white intruders had peaceful intentions, our baby dissolved Guatemalans' suspicions. Many volunteers had to overcome distrust: Were they CIA agents, fugitives from justice, runaways, shirkers, or shysters of some sort? But our baby's presence helped ease the minds of Guatemalans. We were seen as just another family living among them.

Our beautiful daughter, Susana Maria, better known as "Susie," with her blue eyes and light-colored hair, was a special attraction to the local people, a door-opener to the hearts of family-loving Guatemalan women. When Pat walked down a Guatemalan street with Susie in her arms, the local women would pour forth from their homes to have a closer look at the "Gerber baby," as they called her. Susie bore a striking resemblance to the infant pictured on the boxes of baby cereal that they had seen but could rarely afford. Pat made use of the Guatemalan women's interest in Susie to introduce child nutrition and related infant-care projects. As for myself, my huge stature, by Guatemalan standards, became much less menacing when I could be viewed as a "daddy."

Guatemala City, the capital and most modern city in the country, was an assignment for which I was poorly suited. I grew up on a dairy farm in Wisconsin and disliked city life. We were stationed in Zone 3, possibly the worst slum in the capital, a grim shantytown built by impoverished people in the deep ravines known as *barrancas* that fringed the city. Desperate people from the rural areas poured into the capital looking for work and better lives.

They were forced to squat on public land where they erected dwellings out of whatever materials (old doors, cardboard boxes, etc.) they could scrounge up. They carried water great distances. Electricity was rarely found and flush toilets were an unsubstantiated rumor. In that grim neighborhood, Pat and I roamed, often long after dark, with no fear and virtually no sense of where to begin the campaign to improve living conditions and instill hope in "Colonia Trinidad."

On our Peace Corps volunteer reunion visit to Guatemala in August of 2005, Pat and I learned how much more dangerous the sprawling capital city had become. The gangs who now shoot it out in the streets were not around when we served in Guatemala. But I suspect that even back in 1964 there was more danger than we realized.

We were naïve and in denial about anything that might deter us. We had virtually no financial backing for large-scale development projects, so we dabbled in teaching English, finding a place suitable for a community center, showing free movies at a public location, and trying to get to know people and gain their trust. Pat was more successful than I at interacting with Guatemalans. She is gregarious and comfortable in an urban setting. It's challenging enough for me to make conversation in my native language. Doing it in Spanish, with which I was totally unfamiliar before our Peace Corps training began, was like watching a hippopotamus on ice skates. The results were unpredictable.

I admit I spent too much time being angry at Guatemalan men for their displays of *machismo*. When Pat and I went places together it was normal for local males to leer at her, make lecherous comments, and even lower their heads to the sidewalks to look up her skirt while she rode her bicycle. It made me furious and impeded my usefulness. Looking back on such incidents nearly fifty years later, I realize I was foolish to allow obnoxious displays of masculinity to upset me. But I did, and anger is not conducive to helpfulness. Other than helping a few *barrio* families to obtain and salvage wormy sacks of bulgur wheat from CARE, which the slum dwellers cleaned and baked into bread, and the friendly relations I had with a handful of young men whom I taught English in the evenings at our home, I accomplished virtually nothing. Of course, my expectations were extravagantly high, so I became demoralized and impatient to be relocated to a site where the hopelessness was not so eternal.

I was thankful that we were asked to move to Colonia Santa Fe, at the end of the capital's international airport runway, to work with the YMCA on local children's projects. Anticipating the birth of our baby, we found a small house within walking distance of the local bus line. In Santa Fe, poverty was less desperate than in Trinidad and the prospects for useful development seemed brighter. The dwellings were more substantial and the residents were not merely squatters.

Santa Fe's residents were by no means prosperous. An experience I had soon after arriving made an indelible impression on my mind of their hand-to-mouth existence. One night just before teaching my English class, I walked across the street from our rented bungalow to buy a pack of cigarettes (Marlboros, the coffin nails of real men). When I reached the little *tienda* at the end of the street and made my request, the store owner seemed astonished. She was accustomed to selling cigarettes individually, and had no full packs to sell. Nor could she conceive of such prodigal spending. The experience was a useful reminder to me of the poor-as-a-church-mouse lives of our hosts.

During our stay in Colonia Santa Fe, Pat and I each had our own projects. Mine included teaching our neighbors, and anyone else receptive, ultra-modern animal husbandry. I hoped to demonstrate how to raise egg-laying White Leghorn hens to supplement our hosts' meager incomes and diets. I devised a working model of efficient egg production and hoped to encourage the local folks to raise their own pedigree chickens in wire cages that would allow all poop to fall to the ground. A galvanized sheet metal roof over the adjoining cages would keep the birds dry during the rainy season. The floors of the cages, twenty-four in all, were slanted to allow eggs to roll into a trough outside the cages. There, children could gather them without having their hands pecked by irate hens. CARE could be relied upon to provide at least the initial supply of chicken feed — wormy bulgur wheat unfit for human consumption.

I was puffed up with pride at my chicken coop's simple design, ingenuity, inexpensive cost, and compact nature, and convinced that all who observed it in production would yearn to copy it for their own profit and improved nutrition. While I was constructing the coop, Pat and I raised White Leghorn chicks in our home. We put newspapers on the floor, enclosed the drop zone, heated the enclosure with a light bulb, (yes, we actually had electricity) and kept the self-dispensing feeder full. Risa, the cute German Shepherd puppy I bought Pat for her birthday, was smitten by her feathered companions and studied them long and often.

We raised the chicks until they were no longer cute and then transferred them to their cages. I then marked time until eggs became Guatemala's principal export. I invited neighbors to view the kind of "Yankee ingenuity" that had made the United States the promised-land. But I did not anticipate the reaction. It turned out the Guatemalans had a preference for brown-shelled eggs. I had made a fundamental mistake! I had failed to take into account crucial cultural realities, the dietary preferences of the local people. They were no more disposed to eat white-shelled eggs than they were to eat sauerkraut or bagels with cream cheese. My unfamiliarity with their eating habits had doomed my project. When we left Guatemala at the end of our service, I gave the chicken coop and chickens to our fellow volunteer and friend, Bob Kerberlein, who stayed in Guatemala for an additional year of service after our group left the country. He told me in 2005 at our Peace Corps reunion that his villagers wouldn't eat the eggs either. Ultimately they ate my stringy chickens, a dining experience they compared to eating rubber bands.

During our stay in Colonia Santa Fe, I soon had a group of young men studying English under my tutelage. After seeing my height (6' 3") and gorilla-length arms (37"), they decided I would be the most impregnable goalie ever on their soccer, or "futbol," team. I had played North American football, but soccer requires very different skills. I could advance and control a ball with my feet with all the skill of a pregnant cow on roller skates. They assured me, however, that as a goalie I'd merely have to block the opponents' shots and my height, long arms, and huge hands would prevent any team of normal human beings from scoring in my lifetime. I was given the impression that I would be utterly invulnerable, even if I had the foot speed of a maple tree. Under game conditions, their expectations proved unrealistic. I must have disappointed my teammates, but they tolerated my ineptitude with graciousness and our shared efforts bound us together and gave us much to talk about.

Andy Hernandez, the Peace Corps director, allowed us to use his jeep at the end of June when he had to go back to the United States, so Pat could get to the small clinic where she would have our baby. The day after Pat and I had moved to Colonia Santa Fe, she gave birth to our daughter. We were lucky to have that little sky-blue jeep at our disposal when Pat went into labor. It was a Sunday and bus service was even more sporadic than usual on Sundays. Being unfamiliar with labor pains and suffering from amebic dysentery, Pat initially thought her stomach pains were caused by that Peace Corps volunteers' habitual affliction. She insisted that I drive her to the Peace Corps doctor's house to see if he could give her medication for dysentery, then agreed to go to the clinic after learning he wasn't home. When we got downtown, I parked outside the clinic. Pat insisted that I find her some breath freshening Chiclets chewing gum, a staple product of the country, sold on the streets by countless poor boys, before she would go inside. I wasn't happy with her as I roamed through the city's streets searching for a Chiclets vendor. I finally found the gum at a corner stand, took it to Pat, and we checked into the clinic. We were still under the impression that Pat was sick, not in labor.

I took a seat in the tiny waiting room while Pat was escorted inside. I could not have been seated for more than fifteen minutes when a nurse arrived to congratulate me for becoming a father. Still stunned by the news, I entered Pat's room where she lay looking absolutely radiant. Some mysterious chemical change within her body had caused her hair to change to a red color that I had not seen on her before, nor ever since. In her arms was a baby girl untroubled by all the fuss.

As parents, our lives changed dramatically. Having a baby to show off and talk about with family-oriented Guatemalans was our most useful resource in gaining their acceptance and trust.

Pat and I made the best of our stay in Colonia Santa Fe, but our Peace Corps and CARE supervisors understood that we much preferred an assignment in a rural area to one in the capital city. In the scenic mountain region northwest of the city lies an Indian village named San Juan Comalapa. There, three of our Group II predecessors had initiated thriving projects that deserved to be continued after their departure. Pat and I were asked if we'd like to visit the village and consider continuing the projects. We jumped at the chance. Or, it may be, that the truth of the matter is that I was eager to go there and that Pat, always game, showed enthusiasm just to keep me happy.

We visited Comalapa, liked what we saw, and decided to work there. The three Group II volunteers then working among the Cakchiquel-speaking Indians of the region were Bonnie Wey, Jim Noble, and Ron Venezia. Each was an effective volunteer and a hard act to follow. We moved to Comalapa before Bonnie, Jim and Ron returned to the States. The three of them shared an old adobe house with thick walls and a tile roof built in the traditional style with rooms abutting the street and a patio in the center. The three of us moved in with them. Our house had doors large enough for horses to enter and exit the patio, which was overgrown with grass (a great place for my chicken coops). In addition to chickens, ducks and dogs, there was often a horse or two grazing there. The kitchen, bedrooms, storage room, and meeting room were laid out in an L shape flanking the street. Our home was the local gathering place.

Pat continued Bonnie Wey's programs and began working with the women in nutrition and child care. Susie was invaluable to her projects. She was growing faster than the Indian babies, whose mothers were accustomed to feeding their babies breast-milk alone until the next child came along.

My principal responsibility was to oversee construction of a concrete block warehouse to be built by the agricultural cooperative that Ron Venezia and Jim Noble had launched. In the process, I came to regard the Mayan Indians as the best people I had ever known. I learned much about their customs and eccentricities. For example, soon after the Group II volunteers left the village, I called a 7:00 p.m. meeting of the cooperative at our home. When the appointed time arrived, not a soul except me was present. I was shattered. In my discouragement I confided to Pat that I appeared to have failed in my efforts to sustain interest in a very worthwhile project. She tried to comfort me and urged me to be patient. By 7:15, I was inconsolable, trying to imagine how I had alienated such good people so quickly. Around 7:30 p.m. the first members of the cooperative began to arrive, and by 7:45 p.m. the room was full.

I learned a valuable lesson that night. North Americans prefer to live by rules of punctuality that do not apply in indigenous Guatemala or in Latin America on the whole for that matter, though cultural habits are changing. We North Americans associate tardiness with moral failings like laziness, irresponsibility, and lack of discipline. Other societies have more casual attitudes toward the time clock. In fact, no Native American peoples even had any expression for being "on time," nor measurements for small units of time known to us as "hours," "minutes," or "seconds." Furthermore, Spanish culture with its traditional daily "siesta" and its leisurely pace of life, was far less hurried than Anglo America's more industrialized, punch the time-clock approach. Ben Franklin defined "time" as "money," capturing the essence of Anglo American values.

In Latin American and Native American societies there are quite different value systems and viewpoints, with their own historical and cultural underpinnings. We in the United States ought to make a greater effort to understand them without making critical judgments about the people who observe them. Besides, the rat race that we North Americans find ourselves in is destroying our civility, depriving us of the opportunity to savor life, and threatening human relationships. That's a big price to have it our way.

Thanks to our Peace Corps predecessors in Comalapa, the village agricultural cooperative was a thriving organization. Members built a *bodega,* or warehouse, to store crops produced by members until prices were more favorable because of reduced supply. I searched for a competent local mason to lay the concrete block for the exterior walls of the warehouse. The cooperative authorized me to pay the mason one *quetzal* per day, the equivalent of one U.S. dollar. I had no trouble hiring the mason recommended by the cooperative, and he was satisfied with the pay. He proved to be, like countless other

Guatemalan laborers, both in their own country and in the States, hard-working, skillful, and resourceful. The warehouse was completed and opened for business before Pat, Susie, and I left Comalapa.

My dear wife and I were finally in the right Peace Corps assignment in Guatemala. To be sure, the living conditions were Spartan, but we expected nothing more. Our home, with its grass patio, overflowing with chickens, ducks, rabbits, and assorted other critters, was a gathering place for Comalapans. Pat and I had living quarters with dirt floors, sporadic cold water, electricity a few hours each day, and none after 6:00 p.m. The kitchen facilities consisted of a small sink and a wood "stove" made of adobe, open at one end, with a cast iron top. Baking was done by removing the hot wood ashes and sliding a pan in the open end. The nights in the mountains were Siberia-like. I rigged up a shower but its freezing cold water could be endured only when bellowing and shrieking in a voice prohibited by proper social etiquette. Pat could not be persuaded to endure the icy water. She took sponge baths with heated water. Susie had her first bath in a real bathtub in the Palace Hotel in Guatemala City when she was a year old.

Speaking of water, we never found piped water in Guatemala that we regarded as safe to drink. Drinking water had to be boiled for twenty minutes. Instead, we drank bottled water, soft drinks, or beer, my favorite being Gallo. I have forfeited my credentials as a native of Wisconsin , inasmuch as I now drink less than a 55 gallon drum of beer annually, but Pat continues to drink Coke for meals, a habit she acquired in the Peace Corps.

Because we couldn't let Susie crawl around on the dirt floors or in the patio where our menagerie of animals pooped and piddled, I built her a play-pen with a wood floor in the patio. It was rectangular, about six feet long and four feet wide with bamboo posts and rails. Susie stood in it most of each day, holding on to the railings and looking around in wonder, except when she was being carried around in a *reboso* [shawl] by Pat or in the arms of a Guatemalan Indian woman, all of whom regarded her as their own. Today we know what we did not appreciate back then: crawling is essential to a baby's motor development. Unfortunately, the playpen which Susie loved kept her from crawling. She never became as athletic as her younger sister who was born just after our return to the United States. I've always felt a bit guilty about my role in preventing Susie from crawling.

Pat, with her natural gregariousness, was effective in interacting with the people of Comalapa, even though she had to rely on an Indian translator, the talented artist Francisco Telón. Few of the Indian women spoke much Spanish. Most of the men, on the other hand, knew enough Spanish to function in the *Ladino* world, so I had an advantage over Pat in communicating with the natives. But, I confess, she was still better at it than I.

Somehow I had success gaining the trust of the Indians, who were distrustful of European-Americans given the tragic history of their victimization by intruders. On one occasion, in the middle of the night, there was a knock at our door. A young and nervous Indian man explained in fractured Spanish that his wife was in labor and having problems. He hoped I could drive them to the Berhorst Clinic in Chimaltenango, where she could receive first-rate medical attention. We all jumped into our Peace Corps pickup truck, sped through town and down the narrow, dirt, mountain road replete with sharp switchbacks and precipitous drop-offs.

Well before we reached our destination, the mother-to-be gave birth on the floor of the zigzagging delivery room. Of course, her dutiful husband-obstetrician had covered the birthing process with a blanket. But the newborn baby's full-lunged cries announced his arrival. When we arrived at the clinic, a team of nurses hauled off my passengers, and my job was finished. I have savored ever since the memory of my role in the Chevy maternity ward.

On another occasion, a worried Indian farmer knocked on our door in the wee hours and told me his pregnant cow was having difficulty giving birth. Perhaps he had observed my long arms and felt that if anybody could reach inside his pregnant cow and pull out the distressed youngster, it would be the ape-armed outsider in his village.

With my arm inside the pregnant cow I could tell that one of the calf's legs was askew, preventing it from sliding smoothly out of the birth canal. By repositioning the leg, I brought about an uneventful birth. No one was more surprised at the result than I. My father had performed similar procedures on pregnant cows in our dairy herd back in Wisconsin, but I had only observed. My encounter with birthing in Guatemala was representative of the whole Peace Corps experience. Virtually all of us were called upon to do things that tested our creativity and resourcefulness.

In the midst of our work in Comalapa, Pat and I managed to squeeze in a memorable trip to Mexico. Fellow volunteers, Betsy and Mike, who had their baby about four months after Susie, cared for her in exchange for comparable services on our part. Bob

Keberlien, another volunteer from Wisconsin, accompanied us to Mexico for an unforgettable trip.

Part of the trip was made on a second-class Guatemalan "chicken bus," the transportation of the masses. Guatemalans would sit packed in such buses, often with a pig on their laps, a chicken on their heads, and a sick child throwing up down the back of their shirts or *huipiles* (blouses). The top of the bus was likely to be crammed with farm produce (oranges, avocados, garlic) or animals peeing down the windows of the careening vehicle.

Our driver performed his duties with the supreme confidence of one under divine protection. On top of the dash board he had placed statues of St. Christopher, Christ, the Blessed Virgin, his patron saint and the one of his village. Candles, flowers, and assorted religious artifacts completed the ensemble. Under such protection he drove totally devoid of fear. From time to time, he screeched to a halt to run with a big empty can to the nearest stream or water fountain to fetch water for the overheated engine. Passengers were utterly indifferent to the driver's activities, whether he was filling the radiator, fixing a flat, retrieving fallen cargo, or stopping to pee. The passengers merely prayed to reach their destinations. It was a religious pilgrimage.

Seated as I was, right behind the driver, where there was more leg room than in any other seat on the bus, I was afforded an unobstructed view of every inch of the impossible roads over which our conveyance hurtled. There is no possibility that I will ever forget the experience. I needed a vacation in Mexico, if only to recover from our trip there.

Our visit to Mexico City in 1964 was among the happiest experiences of our long journey. We relied heavily upon John Wilcock's 1963-1964 edition of Mexico on 5 Dollars a Day, which cost a mere $1.95 then. Fortunately, we were able to borrow a copy. In Mexico City, then the Paris of North America, we pigged out on hamburgers, french fries, root beer and all the old familiar agents of health destruction that we Americans relish and that Pat and I had done without for too long. Pat found wonderful chocolate in Mexico, the place of its origin. We visited the famous Museum of Anthropology, went to the Ballet Folklorico, watched a game of jai alai, attended a bullfight, strolled through Chapultepec Park, visited the zoo, window shopped, and meandered along the city's tree-lined boulevards with their fountains and outdoor cafes.

We even managed to eat at one or two of the finer restaurants, including Chalet Suiza on Thanksgiving Day. Mexico City was back then a truly beautiful and cosmopolitan center with a thriving cultural life. That visit gave birth to our life-long interest in Mexico and exemplified the cultural broadening that enriched the lives of so many Peace Corps volunteers. Pat and I also remember fondly our visit to Oaxaca, the Indian town where black pottery is made, and our tour of Monte Alban, the pre-Columbian archaeological ruin high outside the city. We sat in the sidewalk café of the Marques del Valle Hotel sucking up the ambience that existed before North American "hippies" discovered lovely old Oaxaca and transformed it. I have noticed that many of the pristine spots that Pat and I have visited, both in Mexico and in the States, were later discovered to their detriment. Such was the case with Jackson Hole, Wyoming, Telluride, Colorado, San Miguel de Allende, Mexico, and other once-charming getaways. More than any other such place ruined by overcrowding was our lovely old Mexico City.

Like most Peace Corps volunteers of our era, Pat and I returned to the United States with mixed feelings about our service. On one hand, we had not accomplished even a fraction of what we had imagined at the outset. Our unrealistic expectations had set us up for disillusionment. On the other hand, we realized we had been privileged to participate in a life-altering experience. We had interacted with, even made lifelong friendships with people in another country. Our projects touched peoples' lives and often made a lasting impact. Pat and I, for example, helped a bright Indian boy from Comalapa come to the United States in a foreign exchange program. He later attended medical school in Guatemala, one of the first Indians admitted. His life and those that he has touched will never be the same.

More obvious to us was that we were by no means the same people who had left our native country just a short time earlier. Nor would we ever be the same again. Our perspectives on the world had widened and deepened. We had seen the toll taken on human beings by grim poverty, the lack of political freedoms and economic opportunities, and enduring exploitation. It was sobering. We were more apt to be appreciative of all that we Americans have, and more disposed to preserve it. That in itself was a result that made it all worthwhile.

LIFE IN THE VILLAGE OF QUESADA

By Bob Hetzel

In so many ways, Quesada was the fulfillment of an idealized image of what Peace Corps life would be.

It had charming adobe houses built around a town square, the church on one end and the school and mayor's office on the other. The people were gracious and greeted us warmly with open arms and big smiles. Our one-room stucco house had wooden shutters. There was a well with a rope and bucket in the backyard. It was right out of a recruitment brochure.

Then night came, and so did the rats. The charm faded as we listened to the rats scurrying across the beams of our half-ceiling. We waited for the plop of one falling on the floor. Then I would grab a flashlight and a broom, open the door and chase it out. Until the arrival of our cat, Mish, we slept in nervous anticipation of the nightly ritual. And we conducted the flea check, not unlike our forefathers, the chimps. With the construction of a shower, we washed away the flea problem, and our cat took care of the rodents.

Another challenge was adjusting to a new concept of time. At our first meeting with the mayor about the school-lunch program, he suggested we hold a town meeting to get volunteers to help. After agreeing on the day, I asked what time we would meet. The mayor replied, "in the evening." Of course, I wanted to know what hour in the evening. He looked at me as if I was a little slow and repeated, "in the evening."

It did not dawn on me that I was the only one wearing a watch. We learned that "in the evening" meant after supper and that the meeting would start when everybody arrived.

One of the great gifts we received from our village hosts was learning that time doesn't have to be measured by the hour and minute for the world to work. Daily life takes on a much more natural pace when there are only three times — morning, afternoon and evening. Things begin when it seems right to begin, and they end when it seems right to end. Life took on an unhurried pace and lasted two wonderful years.

SERVICE IN GUATEMALA

By Tim Kraft

If the Kennedy "vigor," excitement, and challenges didn't touch at least a part of every individual in my graduating class, then I probably hadn't known them very well. A lot of conservative, apolitical grads were on their way to law school, med school, MBAs, and more scholarships. That's not a value judgment — to each his own.

I knew, immediately and with total certainty, when the Peace Corps program was announced, that it was what I wanted to do.

My application was accepted and I was assigned to Guatemala III. We all reported to Las Cruces, NM in September, 1963, to train at New Mexico State University.

The people who stayed through training and went to Guatemala proved to be an intelligent, resourceful, motivated group who would work hard and form lifetime friendships.

Training was intensive, but language classes aside (240 hours in 10 weeks), not very helpful. We slogged through the lectures on political science, Guatemalan history, poultry farming, hog vaccinations, dam construction, and personal health care. We went through the outward-bound-type training and the batteries of psychological tests and interviews, and I suspect we all wondered at the end just what in the hell am I going to do as a volunteer in rural community development in Guatemala?

I lived in the small island town of Flores, located in one finger of Lake Petén Itza, the country's largest lake. People commuted to the mainland by dugout canoe, fitted with old Mercury and Johnson outboards. It was five cents a crossing.

Carol Bellamy and I began by working with a government development agency, Fomento y Desarollo del Petén [Promotion and Development of the Petén], aka FYDEP, on the CARE school hot-lunch program. Thanks to FYDEP (which had storage and distribution capabilities), it was going well.

I began another project working with Sanidad Publica [Health Department] in San Benito, to build, promote, sell, and deliver concrete latrines. For several months I helped FYDEP workers build the concrete bases: assemble the frames, place reinforcement, shovel in the wet cement and trowel it off. It was hot, hard work. But it paid enormous dividends in the friendships and alliances that developed with the workers, who came from the three lakeside towns. It seemed to impress management that I was not there to walk around with a clipboard. A jeep or truck was not hard to borrow because they thought I would put it to good use.

My house in Flores ($15 a month rent) was small, clean, and right on the lake shore. The back "porch" was a partitioned-off area for a hammock, with a wooden trap door and steps that led to the dugout canoes tied up in the back. With a snorkel and cheap spear gun, I could patrol a large area for *blancos*, a silver and black striped fish that fried up pretty well on a small stove. The water was clear, and for all I knew, clean.

128

The town generator provided *luz* (electricity) from dusk until 10:00 p.m. I had an indoor shower and commode, but no refrigerator or hot water. Didn't really miss them.

I rarely left the *Petén* and only then by hitching a ride (up and back) with a FAG (Fuerza Aero Guatemalteco) flight. Work, exploratory trips by jeep and canoes, bar hopping, poker, football, basketball, weddings, quinceaneras [a rite of passage for 15-year-old Hispanic girls], Saints Days, fiestas — these were my diversions and they helped me learn Spanish and become a part of the community.

The second year was devoted mostly to two community projects, the planning and building of underground concrete water cisterns to catch rainwater from church or school roofs.

The small, very poor *aldea* (village) of San Antonio had a good school teacher who helped organize the *mana de obra* [labor] for the excavation next to the school. They did it with shovels — no backhoe.

My FYDEP friends provided the skilled labor on the frames, rebar and concrete for the sides and floor of the cistern. I managed to get enough money out of AID for a pump ... and, by god, we had a cistern.

At no solicitation of mine (it was probably FYDEP), the U.S. Ambassador came up to inaugurate the town's new water system. The guys I worked with made great sport of the *"Alianza Para el Progreso"* sign that AID stuck in the ground. With the dual meaning of *"para"* in Spanish, the sign could also be read, "the *Alianza stops* Progress."

I cannot begin to "sum up" the two years spent in one of Central America's true "last frontiers" — the people and place that is El Petén, the vast rain forest that is the northern third of Guatemala and, in the '60s, home to less than one percent of the population.

There are stories, letters, and notes in my Peace Corps file, and they can't convey the likes of Erwin Ortiz, Julio Molina, Doña Marta or others. I tried to get some of it into "The Fight," a story that needs a lot of work.

At the end of our tour as Peace Corps volunteers, in August, 1965, John McLeod, Bryce Hamilton and I decided we wanted to see the "rest of the place," meaning we would head down the Central American Isthmus and then down the west coast to South America and back up the east.

We almost did the whole thing. From August to November we explored 14 countries, mostly overland, going by cars, pickups, trains, cattle trucks, buses, and boats. Starting with just about $1,000 apiece, our Peace Corps mustering-out pay, "economy" was the watchword (actually I seem to remember another watchword, but we'll leave it at economy).

We saved a lot by not flying country to country. On the other hand, the not-so-user-friendly Latin borders of the 1960s made just about every crossing a hassle.

Another economy was lodging. If there was a beach, we'd camp on it; a night train or boat, we'd board it; a PCV apartment, use it; a PCV recommendation for a cheap hostel or hotel, we'd take it; a bar with rooms upstairs, we'd, well, check it out.

Our trip was cut short after about a week in Rio, when draft notices from home were catching up with us. We had to fly from there to Lima and Panama to drive back to Guatemala and then return to the States.

COMMUNITY DEVELOPMENT IN LAS QUEBRADAS

By Sue Pitt

Following the Peace Corps' strategy of "community development," I involved the women of my village of Las Quebradas in a mothers' club. CARE provided dietary supplements of powdered milk, cheese, and bulgur wheat for the pregnant and lactating mothers. Together, club members sterilized the bottles and prepared the milk. The effort was something of a nuisance to a nursing mother, but not if her breast-fed infant's hunger was satisfied.

We also experimented with feeding the infants Heinz baby food. At our meetings we discussed the pros and cons of using Heinz foods to supplement infant and toddler diets. The women loved our meetings and took our dietary experiments a step further by planting vegetable and fruit gardens. I learned how the seeds of an idea could grow.

Meanwhile, my husband, Bob, convinced the men of Las Quebradas that fertilizer given to him by CARE would improve their corn yields. It truly did make a substantial difference.

Fortunately, everything grew: children, corn, vegetables, and the people themselves. The men formed a Comite Pro-Construccion de Escuela (school construction committee). With the guidance of the Peace Corps' community development strategy, the men of our village built the finest adobe school in the entire Department of Jutiapa.

Our work in Las Quebradas convinced me that people have the need and desire to participate with their fellow human beings to create something larger than themselves.

THE AMBASSADOR WHO NEVER "MIXED IT UP" WITH OUR GROUP

By Ann Silverman

For part of our period of service, Ed Nef, a foreign service officer for whom I had previously worked while a clerk-typist at the Peace Corps' Program Development Office in Washington, was assigned to the political desk at the U.S. Embassy in Guatemala City. At that time, the embassy was still located in Zone 1, in the heart of the city.

One day, Ed approached me with the suggestion that the ambassador, John Edward Mein, might like to meet informally at a social gathering with some of the Peace Corps volunteers. Would it be possible, he asked, for the ambassador to be included in a PCV party? I mentioned this to Jennie, the Peace Corps office secretary, who frequently hosted get-togethers at her apartment when PCVs were in the capital. Her unhesitating reply was, "No way! I'm not having the ambassador come and throw a wet blanket on any party of mine!"

I had inferred from Ed's request that the ambassador's attitude toward the Peace Corps was none too positive, and that this was Ed's attempt to try to soften him up. I lamely, and naively, suggested to him that since a lot of PCVs frequented the Chinese greasy spoon on Sexta Avenida right near the embassy, the ambassador might stop in there sometime on his lunch hour and join a table. It never occurred to me that this would have contravened the embassy's strict security practices.

In the end, no meeting, social or otherwise, took place. And despite very heavy protection, Ambassador Mein was assassinated in 1968 outside the Consulate on Av. Reforma, becoming the first U.S. ambassador killed while serving in office.

THE DAY BEGINS

By Mary Hammond Cordero

I remember the start of each day in Guatemala. The first sound was a knocking by one of the mothers' club members on the metal door of our empty garage. It echoed throughout the house. "*¿Seño, no me regalas la leche para hoy?*" ("Miss, could you give me the milk for today?")

As the mother scurried off to prepare the milk for needy neighborhood children, a cow bell and small hooves could be heard proceeding down the street. "*¿Leche de cabra, no quiere leche de cabra fresca?*" ("Goat's milk, don't you want fresh goat's milk?") Then, goats bleated and took over the dirt street, often bumping the metal door of my bedroom, which fronted the "sidewalk," sending even more dust underneath. The goats calmed down when the herder stopped to milk one of them for a neighbor who appeared at her door with a cup to fill.

I remember going to the kitchen to light the paraffin stove, which prompted one of the mice that lived in that cabinet (most of the time) to pop out and stare at me as if to say, "You're making too much noise." He or she disappeared when I put a pot of water on to boil.

The morning bath was the hardest part of the day for me. Our house had neither heat nor a water heater, so bathing involved heating water on the stove and mixing it with cold water to make three basins of warm water. Those I placed on the rough concrete floor of the open shower. I would lather up, then pour the basins over me to rinse off. In the dry season, we took cold showers, then ran into the patio to dry off in the warm sun.

After breakfast, I walked into the street, dusty or muddy, depending on the season, to the bus stop. The odor of the goats lingered in the street along with the smell of wood-stove fires from the houses where fresh tortillas were made each day. At the main paved thoroughfare, the sounds and smells changed. Buses gunned their engines and back-fired up the hill to our bus stop. The smell of diesel fuel permeated the air.

Peseros, or taxis, followed the bus routes but they cost more and offered no choice of seating. Pressing against the smelly bodies of fellow passengers counterbalanced the time saved. On the bus, you were jostled and bumped, especially when standing, but fresh air was more available with the open doors. On taxis or buses, the smells of unwashed bodies mixed with the heavy perfume of women trying to disguise unpleasant odors.

Anyone who has ridden buses or subways regularly has developed a balancing stance. I acquired one rather quickly thanks to bus drivers who started out with a lurch so they could beat other drivers to the next stop. When bus companies had the same route, drivers would race to get more passengers at the next stop, or they would leave you standing at a stop. They flew by at full capacity, stopping only when someone wanted to get off.

I never became accustomed to the smell of bus fumes. Once, I gagged while waiting for a bus at the central market. Bus after bus stopped, then started off, spewing fumes as they pulled away.

Like everybody else, I turned my body, hoping to avoid the blast of fumes, but there was no escape. The stink in my clothes often forced me to change clothes more than once each day.

If I was VERY lucky, I found a seat and no little old ladies would board and glare at me or sidle up looking pitiful, to shame me into giving up my seat. Other times, a young mother would smile at me and move her seated child so I could sit down, with the understanding that the child would sit on my lap. Not a bad exchange unless the child was a toddler in wet smelly diapers, which was the case more than once. I knew the risk and accepted the offer only when I had my arms full of groceries or other purchases so there was no room for a child on my lap.

Morning passengers were mostly going to work — a mix of working men with no concern for daily hygiene, and office workers wearing aftershave lotion and sporting shiny, slicked-back hair. The women wore basic everyday dress for work or the market; others dressed to kill in the latest fashion fad of their country. And there were always the students in clean and starched uniforms looking a little tired or dazed.

The color range for the women's dresses was amazing. Many wore black, day after day, because widows often wore black the rest of their lives. (I thought of my grandmother and how that had probably been the custom in the States during her childhood.) The *indigenas* (native Indian women) wore embroidered *huipils* (blouses). The variety of designs and colors was wonderful! Skirts were woven in designs used only in their village of origin, although there were a few universal designs. I loved the basic dark blue and green fabrics, but my favorite was a yellow and orange design from the coastal region, a much lighter fabric, suitable for the warmer climate.

If I started out after rush hour, the bus was less crowded and I could sit by a window. Those were my more creative days! I learned that riding buses with set schedules allowed me to relax, because nothing I could do would change our arrival time. I spent the time planning my next project, deciding the first exploratory steps once I arrived in the main part of the city. Our role in community development was ideal in this regard. I loved the freedom from obligatory routine and took pleasure in generating ideas.

I remember the mid-day return trip by bus each day. Workers went home for the mid-day meal and *siesta*, a two-hour lunch break. I often stopped at the market to shop. On rainy days, women juggled woven baskets and bags with their fresh, lovely smelling produce, trying in vain to stay dry. The usual people smells on the bus mingled with those of fresh pineapples, mangoes and vegetables.

The last trip of the day was taken after supper. Norma Wilder, a housemate, and I taught English classes four evenings a week at a community center in a neighborhood nearby. Those trips were full of conversations about daily activities and shared ideas for our classes. The walk from the bus stop to the center was a little frightening at first. It was wintertime with shorter days, so we arrived in darkness and walked the dimly lit streets, not aware at first that several establishments offering sexual services were on our route. We almost jumped off the sidewalk the first time a voice from a shadowy doorway invited us in to take part in those services. After that, we found a different route.

One evening at sunset on the bus, I was admiring the exquisite color changes in the sky — orange and yellow and pink. It made me think about how my family had trained me to live in the here and now. Not a bad idea IF you also hang on to some special memories. So from that day on, I began reminding myself to "remember the special moments," when a sight, a feeling or a situation was too important, unique, or delightful to forget and needed to be treasured forever.

MY MOST TRAUMATIC DAY IN PEACE CORPS/GUATEMALA

By Mary Hammond Cordero

Guatemala III was assigned through CARE to help with school and community feeding programs. My community development work was in Zone 5 of Guatemala City, across the street from the local school. Mothers came to the school each day and prepared a sort of milk porridge. CARE wanted the mothers to use less sugar in the porridge. Otherwise, the program ran smoothly and I saw no real role for myself except to organize a nutritional presentation for the mothers' group now and then.

After a while, one of the mothers gained enough confidence to ask, "Why do we have to pay so much for the 'free' milk the padre gives out?"

"How much are you paying?" I asked.

She named a sum equivalent to our quarter. I knew that Caritas had a food distribution program through the local Catholic parishes, but the charge seemed excessive.

I called CARE supervisor Keni Kent and reported the situation. He explained that local priests were allowed to collect "transportation" charges. Keni agreed that the charges seemed high and he talked to his contacts in the Food for Peace office at the embassy. But nothing had changed when I consulted with the mother several weeks later — same charge and now threats of increased costs. She was ready to skip the program altogether and buy milk at the market.

I called Keni again. He said, "You call them. Maybe that will have more impact."

I did, and the Food for Peace officer irately asked, "Where were you the day I came out to Zone 5 and talked to your roommates?" Apparently he had heard rumors of such charges and wanted live witnesses to interview. I agreed to introduce him to my "source," but requested that it be handled very quietly and that he NOT mention my name in his report.

He said, "Yes, of course," and promptly arrived on the appointed day in the *embassy limo*! I was horrified to see the long, black, imposing vehicle in our humble neighborhood. He could not understand my concern since that was his usual means of transportation. I apologized to the mother who, I suppose, hoped that she would be interviewed in the BIG car.

After the interview, nothing changed until one rainy day when I returned home from work and found my roommate, Norma Wilder, most upset.

"Your priest is looking for you and he is NOT pleased. You'd better go over there right away."

I knew Norma had had some disagreements with the priest in her *colonia* and was rather touchy about complaining priests. So I looked to another roommate, Anne Cartwright, who said, "Yes, you are in trouble. He's mad about something and thinks you're to blame."

I went to the parish house and was ushered into the priest's office. He focused his attention on me and declared, "I hope you are pleased that you have caused a ship full of food and clothing destined for poor families in Guatemala to be returned to the United States."

I was dumbfounded at my apparent power and asked for an explanation. He said, "You need to explain what you did!" I explained what I'd heard and how I'd handled it.

"You don't do things that way," he said. "You are much too young and don't understand how the real world works. You should have come to me and we could have settled this issue between us. You didn't need to bring in your superiors."

Priests in large churches with no microphones learn to project their voices with authority and he employed all his skills for my reprimand.

He said he would have to mention this "misunderstanding" to his congregation on Sunday. I asked if I could be there (I really was naïve) but he replied, "No, there might be trouble. You'd better not come."

Now I was to be the focus of mob anger. I cried all the way to the pay phone and called Keni.

"You'll just have to ride this out," he said. "Let's see how things go when you teach your English class on Monday night."

That was NOT the comforting answer I had sought. The boss was not going to bring in the cavalry to save me.

I asked a neighbor friend to attend the Sunday morning service and report back the congregation's reaction, but that didn't happen. I ate little and had nightmares until Monday evening when Norma and I went to teach our English classes. No one mentioned anything about the priest and it all went smoothly. I was let down, yet relieved.

On Tuesday night, the other class came, laughing and teasing, "So you've taken on the priest!" They seemed pleased that someone had challenged the priest and that he was obviously distressed. They were well aware that he had charged too much. He also sold milk to an ice cream company whose trucks everyone in the neighborhood had seen.

The finale came at my bi-weekly consultation with our Guatemalan supervisor in the school of social work. Doña Marta was a faithful Catholic, concerned about what had happened. "If you don't mind, Mary, I'd like to ask a friend at the diocese about this." I agreed.

A couple of weeks later, Marta invited me to her home for the mid-day meal, a special treat, and I was delighted.

"On behalf of the archbishop, Mary, may I thank you for what you have done," she said.

I was startled. Her friend at the diocese was the archbishop. He had been aware of priests who abused the Caritas program, but had never been able to pinpoint a particular parish because the people tended to protect the local priests. Yes, the archbishop had asked that a ship loaded with supplies be returned to the United States, but only until he could reorganize the Caritas transportation and cost procedures.

I learned there are few secrets at an American embassy. The ambassador had apparently asked the Food for Peace officer for information and I had been mentioned in his memo. Through embassy moles, the priest had discovered "the culprit," and thus my dressing down.

OUR EXPERIENCE IN THE PEACE CORPS, 1963-65

By Dave Snyder

Sally and I started out in a Guatemala City program that turned out to be geared to female volunteers. Initially, I was little more than a chauffeur for my wife. (We had a motorcycle.) After two months, we agreed that we needed to go to a rural village if I was going to accomplish anything in Guatemala. The Peace Corps let us choose our village and we moved to San Vicente.

We spent our first five to six months getting to know people in the village and gaining their confidence. Then Sally set up a town library and worked with the women on nutrition through CARE feeding programs.

I got involved in agriculture and communicated frequently with a couple of Guatemala II volunteers who were agriculture experts. I set up a cooperative that remained active until 1999 when several large coffee growers began to sell their crops at lower prices.

While I was there, we built a warehouse and store with U.S. AID money and had an active chicken-raising operation (1,000 to 1,200 chicks at a time). We processed and sold the grown chickens in supermarkets. I also worked with the co-op on a pig project, fertilizer use, and more.

Sally and I also obtained money from U.S. AID to build a five-room school in one of the *aldeas* where we worked.

MY PEACE CORPS SERVICE

By Ashley Smith

Little did I imagine that I would spend my adult life in this "Land of Eternal Spring." It was to be a two-year Peace Corps tour, then out, possibly to Ireland, a still–unfulfilled dream today.

It was a gorgeous clear day at 3:00 p.m., when we arrived in the country. My recollections are fuzzy, but certain things stand out: the bus ride down the Avenida Reforma, the colorful bougainvillea climbing up trees and the walls surrounding homes, the traffic, the numbers of people wearing shoes, the blond heads rushing along sidewalks, a supermarket (what a relief!), and our arrival at the American Club, where we had lunch and met some important people. I remember thinking how unimpressed I was with the club. It was so dreary and cold. Later, we went to the Palace Hotel, our home for the next month, and that did impress me — the big, open living space, the pillars, the comfortable chairs, the friendly people. The people, I was amazed and pleased to see, had such a variety of faces. (One enters a new experience with preconceived ideas that can disappoint or please. I was pleased to feel comfortable with all I saw around me.)

Bernie Engel burst into the hotel one day soon after our arrival. He was eager to tell us about all the women he had seen nursing their infants "all over the place" in public. That impressed me, and to this day I often think of Bernie's reaction when I see a woman nursing in public, a most natural thing to do.

One of our initial tests that first month was to take a trip out of the city. We were divided into small groups (mine was four), given 35 *quetzals* each, and were told to be gone for one week. My group included Jay Jackson, Ramona Whaley, and Bruce Hupp. We went to San Marcos to check out the CARE milk program. How we got there was up to us. Thanks to Jay, we saw a great deal of the country, from the south coast up to Quetzaltenango, from the black sands of Puerto San Jose, where we slept in rope beds on *petates* (sleeping mats) with rats running over the rafters, through lush, hot Mazatenango, up the green mountains through Zunil, to the flea-ridden beds of a *pension* [boardinghouse] in Xela. Ramona and I rebelled at that and found another place. We traveled through the region, beautiful, cold, sunny, yellow with wheat, green with trees, and lovely with streams of clear water. We always split up on the buses, so we could each have a window to see as much as possible. The buses were crowded with pigs, chickens, children galore, and adults.

On one trip to Huehuetenango, part of the floor of the bus was missing. We could see the dirt road rushing past. How did we dare ride on the buses, on narrow, unpaved, winding mountain roads, driven by untrained drivers, often drunk? Once in a while, someone would go up to the driver, whisper in his ear, and the bus would stop. All would get out, men on one side and women on the other, to take care of necessities. I was intrigued, but did not join the evacuation. In minutes, the journey would continue more comfortably.

By February, we were on our way to our sites. I was with Bob Keberlein and Judy Wilkes. Destination: Monjas, Jalapa, in the eastern part of Guatemala. We had all our equipment and hired a "taxi." We were overloaded for sure, which did not faze the driver one bit. The terms "crowded" and "overloaded" did not exist in the vocabulary of drivers. "Always room for more" was their motto. And off we went. For a while, we were on a macadamized road, but then we turned off onto a dirt one, with 365 curves (we counted them on another trip), twisting and turning through the mountains.

We arrived in Jalapa at about 3:00 p.m. We had to meet the authorities: the governor in Jalapa, and later in Monjas, the mayor. After all the introductions, we were taken to what would be our home, a lovely colonial house of about nine rooms, with an inside "patio," a rustic latrine, no water, and a family of five living in what was once a kitchen. We pitched right in to fix things up to our liking and began the business of meeting people and getting involved. It was not easy.

There was a different thought process in Guatemala, a different pace of life and we had to adapt. There was no rush to get anything done. Electricity for the town was not a priority, given that the generator was not working and no one seemed to mind. There was/is a fatalism about life: "Well, that's the way it is, what can we do? Nothing."

Men seemed to be well-dressed: ironed shirts, trousers, boots and hats. They carried pistols and rode horses. The women, in general, wore simple dresses, had no shoes, and often carried a child, with others in tow. They looked tired and unanimated. There were female teachers, store-owners, and a few others who were better dressed.

Not a month went by that someone wasn't killed by machete or pistol, out of jealousy, vengeance, or for money. That grim reality I had a hard time accepting. I couldn't understand the violence. At the same time, there was curiosity among the Guatemalans about us. Kids would stand at my bedroom window watching me clean and organize things every day. The first few days of my English class, 150 people showed up, not to learn English, but to see the teacher. It was a way for me to meet the people of the town.

Movies were shown on the sides of buildings, the projector put up on the roof of a van. We saw Victor Mature in a caveman film. At that event, I overheard a conversation between a couple of fellows. I learned that when a guy was interested in a girl, he would lure her from her father's house and haul her off to the boonies to have his way with her while she was left with the result. I was horrified and saddened.

The market was another experience. I had never seen such big bananas! Later, at the missionary's home, we learned that they were plantains, to be cooked. We had already consumed a number of them raw. Avocados were in abundance and we ate tons, always inventing new recipes. After I left the Peace Corps, it was quite a while before I could eat an avocado. We hauled our water from the river in *tinajas* (large earthen jars) and boiled and filtered it before use. We took our clothes to a swimming pool up the road. The pool had a run-off into a smaller pool where we washed our clothes. There was a cemetery across the river near the pool and someone told me once, as we were chatting at the edge of the pool, that he would not like to live in the house of the caretaker of the pool because of the spirits that came out of the cemetery at night.

I was always happy not to be a native woman in Guatemala, because I felt they suffered a great deal — giving birth in their homes, going out to look for cooking wood, hauling water from the river, living in houses with dirt floors (though very clean, some of them). And, they had to contend with *machismo* (male dominance).

Something that I always appreciated were bus drivers who would do errands for people, such as picking up letters to take to the city or town where they were heading, or dropping off packages. Of course, that would delay the trip, but I thought it was considerate of the drivers.

Bob, Judy, and I decided to visit other volunteers in a town across the mountains from us. We got an afternoon bus from Jalapa to Mataquescuintla in the early afternoon. The bus broke down at the top of a mountain in a place called Los Pinos. It was early still, but darkening. While a remedy was being sought, we went into a smoky house where there was an altar. In front of it, several women were praying for the dead. I had never seen that before.

The woman of the house invited us in and served us *tamales* and sweet coffee. A gentleman from the bus brought in a cheese bread he had bought for his family and shared it with us, a most humble hospitality that impressed me. (So often those with little are more generous than those with much.) We managed to get horses from the community so we could continue our journey down the mountain to Mataquescuintla. We arrived at 1 a.m., surprising Marcia, Bryce, and Nola. We had a great time seeing cockfights, visiting a farm with pure-bred horses, and walking about the lovely village that resembled Switzerland in the summer.

We did not really accomplish much as Peace Corps volunteers in Guatemala. As I look back, I was very young, 21 and 22 years old. What did I know? And I was shy! But we tried, and through the efforts, we made friends. It takes time to be accepted in a new place, and we were from the outside.

Some of the first questions we were asked were, "Are you Catholic?" and "What do you think of Fidel Castro?" (He had been in Jalapa a short while before we arrived.) When we showed people where Guatemala is on a map, there was a deep disappointment that it is such a tiny country. It would have been better not to have shown them.

We had a bit of a social life. A big party was thrown for my 22nd birthday, with *mariachis* at 5 a.m. and a dance with a *marimba* band in the evening. That was when I noticed that young girls had chaperones, mothers, grandmothers, aunts or older brothers, and that everyone went to the *fiestas*. It was great fun. We went in the back of a big truck to a soccer game in Santa Catarina near Jutiapa. I ate my first *mango* there, from the tree. It was delicious. It is a miracle we got back to Monjas safely, as the driver of the truck was quite looped.

I would say that my Peace Corps experience was a good one. I became comfortable with life in Guatemala, beautiful and lush back then and so simple. The population was about three million in the whole country, which was clean and uncontaminated. I learned to slow down and notice things. I realized that I had much to learn from the people I had come to teach. It's an exchange, really, a sharing. The landscape is different around every curve of the road, from soft to harsh. The people are good and nasty, funny and serious, hungry and well-fed, just as in all parts of the world.

Recently, I returned to Monjas for the first time in 46 years. The whole drive out from the city was familiar, hadn't changed much over the years. When we got to Monjas, my husband told me to look for my friend, Amabilia, the owner of a store, while he went to park. It was very diplomatic of him to leave me alone. I went into the store and saw Amabilia with some people. I waited, looking at her and she looked at me and said, "Ashley?"

I cried. I could not speak for the emotion. She had been a huge support and friend to us. We talked a bit and she met Marcio. She told me her brother, Plinio, named a daughter after me. He liked my name. Such an unexpected honor; it was overwhelming. It was a treat to go back. It looked the same but somehow different.

During my Peace Corps service, I learned to eat black beans, speak Spanish, understand the subtleties of the language, make sense of jokes, and make friends all over the place. In short, I learned to live there. And that's good, because I married a Guatemalan and stayed in country! We have three children and they are very happy that they grew up in a country where "life is real." Now they all live out of the country and are comfortable wherever they go in this world. It is still a life full of experiences.

I never fail to marvel at the colorful people of Guatemala, the dress, the customs, their foibles. Living in Alta Verapaz, I find the thinking processes are different. The people have a hard time looking forward, because the future hasn't come yet; planning for tomorrow isn't possible. But, yesterday is understood because it happened and today is more or less clear because it is in process.

Working with the natives is a challenge. It is not an easy place to live — never has been — but one must live somewhere and we live here.

We have been in touch with Peace Corps volunteers on and off since we married. In the beginning, Marcio worked for Shell Oil, with insecticides in Tiquisate. In the region of the south coast, there were a few volunteers. Then life changed and Marcio, with a North American, bought a farm in Bananera. We had the farm until 1971, when it was sold to Delmonte. The region was active with guerillas and very risky. We went to the States until 1974, then returned to Guatemala, where Marcio started a truck body plant. I went back to teaching English and was busy with our two kids. Marcio's factory merged with another one, making kitchen cabinets and other wood furnishings. Guerillas became active in the highlands where we had bought a small farm. In 1982, the factory closed due to economic realities in all of Central America and we moved to Salamá. Although we considered leaving Guatemala, we stayed because I realized that in spite of the serious situation in the country, Peace Corps volunteers had not been pulled out. I figured someone knew things that we didn't and as long as volunteers were here, we would stay.

We had two Land Rovers, one of which we traded for nine cows and a heifer. We grew from 10 liters of milk production to 200 liters and decided to make gouda cheese. We had pigs, hens, cows, and horses. It was a wonderful farm for the kids to experience. Of course, we all learned along the way and worked very hard.

There were Peace Corps volunteers nearby. We lived right along the road, an easy stop for them. There were marvelous times with the volunteers we met. They were just as nice and dynamic as our group was.

From the valley, we moved to a farm in the mountains near Chilasco, simplifying our lives because we had no electricity. There were just the cows and a farm to be built. After a year of hard work, our partner decided to dissolve our partnership.

We ended up in Cobán, Alta Verapaz, where I taught English to get to know people and help Marcio. In 1990, we started a tour business from Cobán north, over really rough roads. We often took North American and Japanese volunteers from our area on trips. We worked years in the tour and hospitality business, going from one Land Rover to four, the whole family involved.

In 1993, we bought what is now Casa D'Acuña in Cobán. We no longer do tours, as things have changed in the region — paved roads, minivan shuttle service — but we offer hospitality and a restaurant visited by people from all over the world! We have a farm with macadamia nut trees, pigs, sheep, organic veggies, and hens laying organic eggs. Peace Corps volunteers sometimes come to see what we are doing.

None of this has been easy. We are working with uneducated people for the most part and it is a huge challenge to teach basic concepts. I feel it is a miracle that we have managed to do what we have done. Guatemala has changed in many ways, but the basic infrastructure is much the same as when we first came, and there are too many poor people. But that is another subject. I am still fascinated by the country, still curious about what's around the next bend, the colors, the customs — the same, but different.

I thank the Lord for all His blessings in our lives and clearly see His plan for me in mine. Who would have known in 1963?

Photo Caption: "Guatemala III Group Photo"
Photo Credit: Carole Oliver and Christine McReynolds

Photo Caption: "Susie, Evelyn And Linda At The Inauguration Of Their Social Center in Barberena"

Photo Credit: Evelyn Glasscock

Photo Caption: "New School Inauguration (Committee Members With Bob And Sue)"
Photo Credit: Sue Pitt

Photo Caption: "Camille And Bob Gilke, Guatemala
III's Senior Married Couple"
Photo Credit: Pat and Dave Smits

Photo Caption: "Tim And Other Project Organizers At San Antonio's New Cistern"

Photo Credit: Tim Kraft

Photo Caption: "Hi-Ho Silver (Bernie Rides Again!}"

Photo Credit: Carole Oliver and Christine McReynolds

Photo Caption: "Dave With Newborn Calf"
Photo Credit: Pat and Dave Smits

Photo Caption: "Pat 'Hangs Out' In Training"
Photo Credit: Pat and Dave Smits

Photo Caption: "Carole And Chris In Their Kitchen"
Photo Credit: Carole Oliver and Christine McReynolds

SECTION III

PEACE
CORPS
WRITERS

.

THEREAFTER

WHO ARE THESE STRANGERS?

By Ramona Whaley

A white-haired woman stands quietly by her car. She scans the scene surrounding her, seemingly searching for something or someone. She is the only person I see in the parking lot.

So, where's my old Peace Corps pal from the early 1960s, who a couple minutes ago phoned for me to come down from my seniors' tower apartment to meet her in the parking lot?

I haven't seen that bubbly, brown-haired vivacious girl with laughing eyes and endless energy for decades. She's not here. But, that quiet elderly lady is still hanging around.

And then, I get it.

I walk over to the senior citizen and into a silent bear-hug that seems to last four or five minutes — one minute per decade since we and other Guatemala III Peace Corps volunteers wished each other "a nice life," then said our goodbyes for nearly forever on our way home to the States in 1965.

I recall another friend describing her surprise when she looked up to see "an old man" ambling toward her at a Guatemala III reunion. Only after looking into his eyes did she finally recognize that once-and-still-very-dear friend of her youth, whom she had been trying to identify among all the strangers gathered there.

After that, she looked first in everyone's eyes. That, she said, was the only way to recognize old acquaintances in new bodies.

"You always know by the eyes," she said.

Still, my mind rebels against accepting as one and the same those familiar dewy-fresh faces of my youth and these aging faces confronting me now. Who are these strangers and what have they done with my young friends?

The aging of my friends hits harder than the cruel honesty of my own mirror. Happily, I have found a fountain of youth where time stands still. It is Guatemala III's transcontinental chat line set up five years ago by fellow Peace Corps volunteer Jay Jackson.

After decades of separation, we reunited via cyberspace. Guatemala III returned Peace Corps volunteers now joyfully spend a lot of time online together. I have identified the contemporary faces of my old Peace Corps gang in group photos taken at our 2003 and 2005 reunions, which I missed.

When our chat-line messages roam late into so many nights, it is Guate III's original but long-vanished faces who keep me company alone at my computer. Excited e-mails fly so fast among us and in my mind's eye I still see those kids' faces I knew back in the early 1960s. Invisibility keeps us ageless.

When we do reunite, the initial stunned reaction gradually gives way to a comfortable familiarity with our alterations. Shared memories erase even the most conspicuous evidences of aging.

Inside our silvery, snowy or bald facades are the same caring idealists who first came together in the fall of 1963, confident that through the Peace Corps we would improve the condition of our planet's suffering peoples. The convergence of two distinct times of our lives (the early 1960s and the early 2000s) makes aging a positive.

We who survived such training ordeals as hanging from Las Cruces mountains, drown-proofing, endless hours of exhausting total immersion in Spanish language studies and the "Selection Out" ogre; we who laughed and relaxed together at our Billy The Kid get-away in nearby Mesilla; we who cried together, heartbroken, at hearing our Peace Corps leader had been shot and killed in Dallas on Nov. 22, 1963; we who worked so hard to promote peace and friendship for the United States in our village sites; we who will celebrate the fiftieth year of the Peace Corps are proving the validity of JFK's third Peace Corps goal. We are still together.

We Peace Corps pioneers of the early 1960s, now in our late sixties or early seventies, will forever be bonded by our Guatemala III experience and our kindred spirit that brought us together in the first place.

We will always be traveling companions. Growing older together promises to be just one more unforgettable adventure. "The best," as poet Robert Browning wrote, "is yet to be!"

WHAT COULD WE POSSIBLY HAVE IN COMMON WITH THESE OLD GEEZERS?

By Dave Smits

The shared Peace Corps experiences that often bond for life volunteers who served together can be the key to a lasting marriage as well. In 2011, as Peace Corps celebrates its 50th year, Pat and I will have been married almost as many years. Many people, upon learning the duration of our marriage, are not sure if they should offer their congratulations or condolences. It seems to me that after forty-some continuous years of doing almost anything legal, a medal ought to be received, if only for stamina. Our youngest grandson, Dylan, eight years of age, who has devoted his young life to uttering the unembellished truth and shows absolutely no aptitude for a career in diplomacy, says that "grammy" and "grandpa" have been married forever. Actually, it has not been that long, though my memory of things that occurred before our marriage is pretty much limited to my elementary and high school years, which I would happily forget.

It's strange that Pat and I have been married for so long, since we are utterly incompatible human beings. Pat is an unabashed extrovert; I am an introvert. She is an eternal optimist; I'm not sure I'll be around to finish this essay. She is a night owl, fond of watching movies into the wee hours of the morning. I'm normally unable to stay awake in my recliner beyond the first ten minutes of the same movie, but out of bed with the roosters. We don't even like the same music. She is able to do at least a dozen things simultaneously. By contrast, a week or so ago I misplaced my pickup truck keys and found myself wandering around the house having forgotten what I had started out looking for. Thus, for me, focusing on even one task is a dying art. As the clinching piece of evidence that we are hopelessly different, Pat eats blue cheese dressing on her salads; I would only eat that evil concoction if there were nothing else on earth to eat — and then I'd regret having done so.

How in the world could two people so different have been married so long? I have no doubt that our Peace Corps experience together, coming as it did so early in our marriage, coupled us in a way that human beings hope they will become bonded to the special people in their lives.

In the summer of 2003, I witnessed a prime example of that bonding at the reunion of our Guatemala III Peace Corps group in Mahwah, New Jersey. Pat and I arrived at the gathering late as usual. This, by the way, is another example of our incompatibility. Pat has never arrived on time for any…Oops, I have nearly forgotten one of the foundation stones of a long-lasting marriage. It is best to keep your big mouth tightly closed on a wide variety of touchy subjects.

When we arrived at last at that 2003 Peace Corps reunion and opened the door to the room in the restaurant where our fellow Guatemala III volunteers were gathered, I saw an assemblage of old-timers who looked much too ancient to be the folks we were looking for! That those aging faces were not familiar, I should not have found surprising. We had seen only a couple of them since leaving Guatemala back in 1965. A few members of our group had remained in Guatemala, but the large majority of us had returned to the United States at the conclusion of our Peace Corps service. Thereafter, we had each pursued our own thing over an extended period of time, or more precisely, for forty years. Our post-Peace Corps years had taken us in many different directions and had been spent in places ranging from Alaska to Colombia, South America and from Thailand to God-knows-where.

What could we possibly have in common with these old geezers? I feared we were in store for a long evening.

Pat and I each helped ourselves to an empty chair and found ourselves in the midst of those fossils whose thinning and graying hair, thickening waistlines, and wrinkled necks and venerable faces contradicted the youthful exuberance that each radiated. They were hugging and kissing one another, laughing like hyenas, and finishing one another's sentences as though they were old drinking buddies.

I am not a person who normally lets his guard down in such situations, but I quickly found myself letting it all hang out and thoroughly enjoying the company of the museum pieces in that room. Reunions too often afford those attending an opportunity to posture and play the game of one-upmanship. There was nothing of the sort going on at this reunion. Those gathered in that room were beyond caring about the impressions that they made on their old comrades. They looked as different from one another as Southern Californians do from Wisconsinites. Some had aged well; others — but why go there? Some were retired; others still held jobs. Some were casually dressed, others in more formal attire. But these differences were insignificant to people who had known humanity in its many poses and guises.

Every former PCV in that crowded room had shared with the others a unique and special experience that outsiders simply could not understand nor adequately appreciate. Those of us in attendance knew deep in our bones that we had all teamed up long ago to do something meaningful — something which had changed our lives and, hopefully, the lives of others for the better. Together we had endured challenges; experienced highs and lows and in-betweens; known frustrations, setbacks, and even a few successes. We had turned to each other for advice, support, encouragement, comfort and companionship. We had enjoyed the sights, sounds, smells and tastes of a lovely little-known country with exotic cultures and hospitable people. Those people yet today occupy a special place in our hearts and memories.

We had partied together and we had — I know it sounds melodramatic, but it's the unvarnished truth — cried together. I'll never ever forget the scene in the dining hall on the campus of New Mexico State University during our Peace Corps training when news reached us of JFK's assassination.

Many of us, especially those who had been inspired by his call to "ask what you can do for your country," wept openly and unashamedly. I don't think any of us were ever quite the same after that tragic event. And it will never be erased from our memories.

We shared those experiences, and much more, in the full bloom of our idealistic and naïve youth. To be sure, there were among us from the outset, a few fellow volunteers already senior citizens at the time, who served as reminders of how we ought to live our lives to the fullest even beyond the prime of our youth.

There is no doubt that we survivors of the adventure were bonded together, a band of brothers and sisters who had shared a defining experience, which in the fullness of time assumed for many of us a growing importance and a deeper meaning.

Besides, as I came to realize only after our Peace Corps service was long over, the people with whom we served in Guatemala III were, on the whole, extraordinary and exceptionally likeable human beings.

Pat and I were indeed fortunate to have stumbled into a humanitarian international adventure in the company of other Americans willing to do their part to improve the lives of less-fortunate people in the Third World. We all know that our accomplishments paled in comparison to our soaring expectations. But each of us, in our own way made an honest effort, at some inconvenience, to look beyond ourselves and do what we could to make this world a better and more peaceful place. Although it may sound theatrical, it's true, and those of us who served in Guatemala III are wiser and bonded to one another for having done so.

And, just as we Guatemala III veterans were linked by shared experiences and youthful idealism, so the same and many other more personal versions of such experiences had united Pat and myself in ways we have no hope of ever escaping. She and I long ago emerged as "we," or as others refer to us, simply "Pat and Dave," with no thought of separating the names.

RETURN TO LAS QUEBRADAS

By Sue Pitt

Forty years after my Peace Corps service — exactly the life expectancy of a Guatemalan when our group served there — it was time for we Guatemala III returned Peace Corps volunteers to go back to Guatemala for a reunion.

Most of my life has involved children: raising my own and teaching others. Educating my own was expensive and my earnings were minimal. So when Guatemala III reunited in New Jersey in 2003, the $900 trip expense was not in my budget. My son was then going to college.

But I was determined to attend the 2005 reunion in Guatemala! I had always wanted to see once again my adopted homeland of Quezada and my people there. But, to be truthful, the civil war and subsequent decades of violence in Guatemala made it too frightening for me to consider going.

The war had begun soon after "Guate III" arrived in 1964. A curfew had been imposed in the capital, Guatemala City. Just before dark, army vehicles filled with Guatemalan soldiers carrying rifles ominously patrolled the *calles* and *avenidas*. Those streets and avenues were vacant, as they were supposed to be under the curfew.

A few times when my husband, Bob, and I left our assigned rural site to go into Guatemala City and sleep on the floor at the Peace Corps office, a Guatemalan soldier stood on guard outside.

We had restrictions on the meetings we held in our own little town as well. If there was going to be a meeting of three or more people (sounds like something from the Bible), we had to obtain permission from our mayor. The mayor had a one-room office on the plaza just a block from our home, so getting in touch with him was not a big deal.

The imposing block-long military headquarters in our *Departamento de Jutiapa* was on the plaza right across from the Spanish Colonial Catholic Church. We would go from the dusty plaza a block away to the small outdoor market and buy whatever fruits and vegetables we could get our hands on and even some of the freshly butchered meat hanging up and covered with flies. We figured if we trimmed it and cooked it well, we would survive just like the rest of the people. We never had a sick day, just some hungry ones.

The curfew and military presence during our time in Guatemala foreshadowed the violence that erupted in the following decades. After returning to the United States, I would scour the news for what was happening in Guatemala. I once read in *Time* magazine that the general who had arranged the transportation of CARE food supplements — flour, bulgur wheat, powdered milk, and cheese — for our town and the thirteen surrounding *aldeas* [villages] was then attacking guerillas in a helicopter raid.

Then, of course, there was the well-publicized hunger strike of the beautiful, Harvard-educated lawyer who sought the whereabouts and release of her Mayan-resistance-fighter husband.

Gruesome details of the military's torturing of Guatemalans and reports of the hundreds of missing persons in the country made traveling there much too scary for me in the years after our return from Peace Corps service. But with the election of Guatemala's current president, I feel an enduring peace may finally be achieved.

After our 2003 reunion in New Jersey, our own Jay Jackson set up a chat line for our group, so we were able to talk via e-mail about plans for the reunion in Guatemala in August 2005. In May of that year, I was camping near Santa Barbara, California, where Norma Wilder, another member of our group, now lives. She was the reunion planner and provided reassurances. I signed up right away. I felt I would be "home" again and safe in Guatemala.

On the first leg of our return trip to Guatemala, we stayed at the renovated Biltmore Hotel in a now-thriving tourist section of Guatemala City. I remembered it from our Peace Corps days as being close to a familiar round-about that I always saw while riding the bus.

Then we were on to Lake Atitlán, the country's most beautiful lake, surrounded by volcanoes, where each village along the shores has its own hand-woven and embroidered costume. In Panajachel, the locals made *tamales* from scratch and I remembered feasting to the tunes of a *marimba* band in that picturesque village. Guatemala III definitely still knew how to party and we shared our memories and brought ourselves up to date on our entire lives. We were exuberant and excited.

The setting for our week's last two days together was Antigua, once the capital of Colonial Guatemala. It is a city filled with the ruins of monasteries and churches and with flowers, fountains and homes with carved wooden doors huge enough to allow the passage of horses and carriages. We dined in one of those monasteries that had been converted into a restaurant. The stairs in the courtyard allowed us to climb up to the roof, where we gazed out at the cityscape by moonlight. The next morning we were whisked away on a minibus — what luxury, compared to the "chicken buses" we had ridden in our Peace Corps days — to the airport to be flown back to our homes and, oh, such different lives.

My real return to Guatemala, however, happened before the rest of the group arrived for our reunion. Traveling with a friend, Mary Visarraga, I went directly to Quezada, my old Peace Corps site, and to one of its surrounding *aldeas*, Las Quebradas. The former is where I worked as a Peace Corps volunteer in the early 1960s, where I lived, breathed and sweated for almost two years. That is where my people were.

My return meant tracking down my old friend, Rosa, first. We had been corresponding ever since I left Guatemala, but she had not answered my last letter. Was she in Jutiapa or Jalpatagua? That was the question.

The search for Rosa began with my trip from Guatemala City to Jutiapa, where she had lived on weekends, when she was not teaching in Las Quebradas.

The bus left us off near the post office in Jutiapa, where we inquired as to her whereabouts. She probably was in Jalpatagua, we were told, but she might be on the outskirts of town.

The only way to find out would be to take a city bus part way and then trudge the rest of the way to Jalpatagua with our backpacks on a hot August day. Another crowded bus took us to Jalpatagua, where we got off and asked the first vendor we saw about Rosa.

Yes, indeed, Rosa was in Jalpatagua. We were assured that she was just four blocks away.

Rosa and her husband, Leonido, lived in a long adobe home with imposing double doors. Inside was a grand patio with growing vegetables, fruit trees, tropical flowers and a parrot.

By now, they had heard we were arriving and Leonido and Rosa were lounging in their hammock watching TV. After knocking on the door, Mary and I were suddenly receiving Rosa's warm embraces — finally, after all these years! ¡Que alegría! [What joy!]

It was an occasion to butcher a chicken and share a meal, then stroll around town, visit friends and relatives, stop by a church and buy tortillas, freshly made over a comal [earthenware griddle] heated by a wood fire. We returned to Rosa's kitchen to eat black beans, tortillas and chicken, served on a table covered with a flowered oilcloth.

We slept in Leonido's and Rosa's bed most comfortably, for they insisted on giving it up to us.

Up at dawn, Leonido milks his cows on the outskirts of town. He is a seventy-year-old retired government worker. His wife is a retired teacher. I have a feeling they do not receive large pensions, for when Rosa went out to buy sweet bread she said that if anyone knocked on the door, a pitcher full of milk was on the table. She sold it for a quarter a cup. Twice there were knocks on the door and I made two sales.

¡Adios Leonido! We were off with Rosa on the morning bus to Las Quebradas. It and Quezada are where my heart really lies, where some of the best days of my life were lived, and where that day would again be one of my very best.

Nobody met us at the bus stop in Las Quebradas on the Pan American Highway, so we walked a mile on that hot August morning in 2005, with our backpacks, Rosa with her sodas in a plastic woven shopping bag.

On a spacious porch across the road from the school, we found mainly women, both elderly and young, cooking school lunches. Also there were two young male teachers and Don Rodrigo, who had served on our school construction committee. I barely recognized him for, of course, he had grown much older, just as I had. He was smartly dressed from sombrero to boots. Don Rodrigo, Rosa and I reviewed for the teachers the history of the construction of their school.

An old dark house with no windows served as a school until eight young men of that community resolved to build a fine new one. They involved my husband and me, their Peace Corps volunteers, in the project.

We told the school's teachers how forty years ago it had been agreed that each man would make and bring 100 adobes to the construction site. Each would also bring 100 pounds of lime gathered from the hills and 100 pounds of sand from the river. As a group, they would cut down and drag to the site as many trees as the project would need for lumber.

We told them how Bob and I obtained help from our friend, Mike Guolee, back in Wisconsin. Mike was teaching at Peckham Junior High in Milwaukee. His students enthusiastically raised $500 through means such as the traditional bake sale. With that money, the committee purchased tin for the school's roof, cement for its floor, laminated windows and two hardwood doors.

The school's teachers of 2005 were eager for their students to hear this history and Don Rodrigo, Rosa and I told it over and over again to the three crowded classrooms of children. Really, it was mostly just me talking. I told them to be proud of their neighbors, because not all communities have men with such determination to improve their children's education. The children understood and gratefully applauded.

With the sound of children's and teachers' applause ringing in our ears and swelling our hearts, we walked down the hill, through a river and past a field to Conchita's.

Conchita was one of the community's life bloods in our Peace Corps days. Isaias, her handsome, fine-featured, dark-haired husband had passed away, but she and I hugged joyfully, as if to say we were still alive and still full of that creative spirit of the sixties.

And, from next door came gentle, happy, Francisco and his wife, and Don Leopoldo walked up the path in an ironed, white cotton shirt and white pants.

Everyone understood that Don Leopoldo was lonely, and everyone expressed genuine sympathy on hearing that I, too, lived alone. "Do they have such feeling for everyone?" I wondered. "Or am I really special to them?" as it seemed to me.

Conchita had made a tasty soup of chicken broth and everyone had some, with one or two potato slices and a sprig of cilantro on top. There were also those delicious corn tortillas that I remember fondly, and a cold soda, for Conchita now had a refrigerator. We learned later that she sells the cold sodas from her refrigerator until 10 o'clock at night.

When the long-awaited fiesta meal was over, I brought out a half-dozen 8 x 12 photographs from my Quezada and Las Quebradas days. One photo, that I always show my own students in my talks about my Peace Corps experiences, and in bank art exhibits, shows the classic Guatemalan kitchen made of poles with spaces in between them.

In the photo, two young women and an elderly, gray-haired woman stand between the poles. On the left is a young girl standing behind a *metate* [grinding stone] made from a slab of black volcanic stone. With a hand-held stone she will grind the corn into flour. On the other side is a raised table called a *fagon*. A fire cooks the clay pot of beans. This is the way women prepare the basic diet of corn tortillas and black beans eaten at breakfast, dinner and supper. Perhaps every other Sunday they will prepare chicken, and in between, some eggs.

I showed this revealing photo to Don Rodrigo and said I believed the woman on the right was from Las Quebradas, and that I knew she had died in childbirth.

He said, "Yes, she was my wife, and the gray-haired woman was my mother. I have never had a photo of my wife to show my first-born son."

I placed it in his hands. "This is yours," I said, to express that I truly understood what he'd just told me.

Tears welled and everyone on the porch gathered around. We couldn't believe what we had just seen happen. How could these people, time and time again, give such fulfillment and meaning to my life?

Did anyone ever envision a connection this strong when the Peace Corps was formed? I know there is a true, personal bond among us and it has made the meaning of all our lives deeper.

I wore the gold medal adorned with blue ribbons that the committee had presented to Bob and me at the school inauguration ceremony when we were in the Peace Corps so long ago. It is engraved "En eternal gratitude por sus múltiplas sacrificias"…"in eternal gratitude for your many sacrifices."

"Look how she cares," they said. "She has guarded it all these years."

I thought to myself, "Thank you for feeling that way about me in the first place and for still loving me."

We spent the night at Conchita's house, which is one long, wide room. A refrigerator at one end holds the contents of her store. At the other end are a TV and two beds, so ornately decorated in the Guatemala City style of lace and ruffles that Mary and I jokingly asked if it's the honeymoon suite. Conchita's kitchen is down the long porch where we had our school committee party earlier that afternoon. It has a raised wood fireplace, a little table and a large concrete sink where water is collected off the roof to wash dishes and clothes. To get to the outhouse, we had to walk down by the cornfield.

Nothing seems to bother Conchita. She knows how to work hard and how to have a really good time. She still remembers that at the school inauguration long ago, we all danced until midnight and enjoyed one another's company.

Early the next morning we were in the back of a truck riding to Quezada with men, women, and children from Las Quebradas. The driver was the son of one of the school committee members, and the mayor's assistant.

We approached Quezada, which never had a single car in town in our Peace Corps days. Now I saw paved streets and street signs. Sleepy Quezada had grown from 1,500 to 15,000 people.

I found my friends and joked around with them.

"Coni," I said, "it is all because you had ten children!"

CONSUELO, MY GUATEMALA CONNECTION

By Evelyn Brubaker Glasscock

In 1981, 16 years after my Peace Corps service, I wrote to my dear Guatemalan friend, Consuelo Urruela, and asked her about the conditions in her country. Was it safe to come back to Barberena, my Peace Corps site in the 1960s? I hoped to visit Guatemala for a couple of weeks, even though there was a guerrilla war still going on down there.

Consuelo wrote back that it was as safe as anywhere. So, in July my friend Linda and I went to Guatemala.

We took a guided tour the first week so Linda could see the country's major sights. We thought that would be the safest way to get around. Then we would spend the second week in Barberena, staying with Consuelo and her husband Arturo.

Even though we would not be going to Barberena right away, Consuelo and Arturo met us at the airport and took us to our hotel in Guatemala City, where we spent the first night and met our tour guide. Linda and I were the only tourists in a 15-passenger van!

We went to Panajachel first, and had our hotel, the restaurants and everything else practically to ourselves. Then we headed to Chichicastenango, where we stayed at the Maya Inn on the plaza.

Early Sunday morning we were awakened by gunfire in the plaza. It continued for some time, as I pushed further and further under my bed covers. I know my footprints are still engraved on the footboard of that bed. We felt uneasy about our safety; our door was only latched with a hook.

Finally, about 6:30 a.m. I took a shower, hoping the sound of running water would block the sound of shooting outside.

Around 7:00 a.m., we ventured outside. By then, the gunfire had ceased. We found sheets of paper everywhere on the ground. They had been left there by the guerrillas, announcing a new Sandinista front being launched in Guatemala, on the anniversary of the Sandinista takeover in Nicaragua.

The market in the plaza was open, but nobody was shopping and the vendors had fear in their eyes. We walked toward the church and saw Guatemalan soldiers assembled. We felt we shouldn't be there, but we shopped a little more, then went back to the hotel, while an army helicopter hovered over the plaza.

Around 10 a.m., we left for Antigua, when the real adventure began.

We had not gone far before we encountered the first obstruction on the highway. The guerrillas had strewn tree branches full of glass and nails across the roads between Guatemala City and Chichicastenango to make it difficult for the army to get from the capital city to the outlying areas. To sweep the road as they went along, all buses had brushes made of leafy tree branches fastened to their front bumpers.

Soon the van blew out its right front tire, and there we were, Linda and I, not far from the place the guerrillas had just attacked.

The driver had pulled over so that the right-side tires of the van were in the sand and the left-side tires on the pavement. Repeatedly, he jacked up the right front tire, but the van slipped off the jack and mired in the sand each time. I suggested putting all four wheels on the pavement, but he ignored me, then five minutes later, gave it a try.

Finally, the damaged tire was in the van, and we were on the road again. The driver said he would stop at the service station ahead to get the tire repaired, because we might need it again before getting to Antigua.

At the service station, we saw that the surrounding parking lot was full of buses, trucks, vans and cars, all with flat tires being repaired. The driver left for a while, then came back and told us we would have to stay a while longer. There was "a problem up ahead," he said, but wouldn't explain.

Linda and I got out the cards and started playing rummy. The driver wanted to play, too, and others stood around watching — two *gringas* in the midst of all the vehicles and people, oblivious to the "problem up ahead." Ignorance is bliss!

Finally, the drivers decided we would be okay if all the vehicles traveled together in a caravan.

Back on the road, we soon saw the "problem up ahead" — the burned out shell of a Greyhound-style bus. The passengers, tourists, had been taken off the bus and robbed. We were not told where they were.

The road between the service station and Antigua was a major obstacle course. To avoid the piles of branches laced with nails and glass, our driver swerved from one side of the road to the other for four and a half hours until we arrived in Antigua.

Our time in Antigua and the rest of our trip went well. Back in Guatemala City, I bought a *Prensa Libre* newspaper to see if there was any news about that weekend's events in Chichicastenango, and there it was — an article with a picture of the burned out bus shell. The police office in "Chichi" had been bombed and a couple of policemen and several guerillas had been killed.

The next day, when Consuelo and Arturo picked us up at the hotel in Guatemala City, Consuelo said she had been scared to death and had made various phone calls, trying to check on us.

"And you wrote that it was perfectly safe to come to Guatemala, right?" I said, in a joking tone. With a sheepish look on her face, she answered, "Alma and I talked, and we decided that if we told you the truth, you wouldn't come!"

That's my dear friend Consuelo!

We spent the rest of our time in Guatemala visiting with friends in Barberena and going wherever Consuelo and Arturo wanted to take us.

Years later, in the early 1990s, Consuelo was in Amherst, MA, with a group of Guatemalan teachers. When she arrived, she wrote me to tell me where she was. There was a misunderstanding over the appointed meeting time and when we got to Amherst, Consuelo was out shopping. Her friends took us to their apartment and told us to wait there and surprise Consuelo when she got home.

She was indeed surprised.

My friend and I spent the weekend with Consuelo and her roommates. She took one day off from the program she was attending, and we rode into Vermont and other places she wanted to see. It was so good having her in my country and showing her around, even though it was Massachusetts and Vermont instead of my Virginia.

I have known Consuelo since my days as a Peace Corps volunteer in Barberena in early 1964. Consuelo lived across the street and I met her soon after my arrival. A strong bond developed between Consuelo and Arturo, all their family members and me. We spent a lot of time together. I was always welcome in Consuelo's home, and I felt at home with her. She was one of the women in our "*Comite por Mejoramiento de la Communidad*" [Committee for the Betterment of the Community] during our two years there. When we needed eggs, we went to Consuelo's. When we wanted to visit someone, we asked Consuelo to help us.

In August, 1965, when my site partner, Susie [Stapleton], and I left Barberena as Peace Corps volunteers, Arturo came in his car to take us and our luggage to the bus. When we told him we weren't quite ready to go, he gave me his car keys and told me to come downtown when we were ready. When we drove to the center of town, there was such a mob, Arturo decided to drive us out of town to the highway north of Barberena and put us on the bus there.

Consuelo has remained my main connection to Barberena and Guatemala. We have exchanged letters through the years and cards every Christmas.

When I returned to Guatemala in August, 2005, for our Guatemala III Peace Corps reunion, I had two reunions — one with my Peace Corps buddies and one with my Barberena buddies. I spoke with Consuelo the night I arrived. She sadly informed me that Arturo — dear, sweet Arturo — had died the preceding month.

Susie, her husband Bob and I spent two days with Consuelo in Barberena. With Alma, another of our Guatemalan friends from Peace Corps days, and Consuelo showing us around, we reacquainted ourselves with the town.

The day we left, Susie and Bob flew out early in the morning, but my flight didn't leave till 2:00 p.m. Consuelo and her son, Chepe, took me to breakfast and to an *artesanía* [craft shop] full of Guatemalan handiwork and then to visit with family and friends until I left. That was the last time I saw Consuelo.

A year later, on Nov. 7, 2006, I received a message from Chepe headed *"Malas Noticias"* — "bad news." Consuelo had died on Oct. 27, 2006.

I felt as if my tie with all of Guatemala had been severed. Yes, I have other ties there but none as strong as with Consuelo. She was so very special.

Consuelo had told me in 2005 that she wanted to come visit me. Her kids wanted her to come immediately, to help her through her mourning for Arturo. That, of course, made me very happy, because I had tried to get Consuelo and Arturo to Virginia for over 40 years.

At Christmas in 2005, Consuelo wrote that she was coming to the United States and wanted travel advice. I answered all of her questions quickly, but I never heard from her again. I e-mailed Chepe and one of his sisters and asked them to talk to their mom. Again, no response. I heard nothing until the sad e-mail ending a four-decade connection with Barberena and Guatemala that started with my Peace Corps service in 1964.

SIMPLE PLEASURES

By Bob Keberlein

I awoke at 1 a.m. this morning to the sound of roosters crowing and dogs barking. I got up and started to read for a while, but distracting thoughts started floating through my mind. I marveled at the simple pleasures I find here, living the leisurely life of a retiree.

I am back in Guatemala again, at my 1960s Peace Corps site, San Manuel Chaparron, relaxing in the beautiful retirement home we built here on earlier visits during my last years of teaching high school in my native Wisconsin.

The *feria* [fair] ended yesterday. Like any county fair in the United States, the annual feria has lots of games, carnival rides and booths selling all types of foods and other goods. It is set up all over town. If you can imagine a county fair, hectic and noisy, right in the middle of your town, that is what it has been like here these past four days. There was a beer tent about two feet away from my door. The Ferris wheel was about 20 feet away. That made sleep difficult until after 2 a.m.

The weather is marvelous. I have not needed a sweater yet and the evenings are cool enough to dispense with my fan. On my first arrival in Guatemala in January, 1964, with my Peace Corps group, Guatemala III, I was awed by this tropical climate and its unfamiliar plants. I had never experienced a warm climate.

Flying into Guatemala City for my most recent visit, arriving there at 6:25 a.m. on Thursday, March 6, 2008, I had wanted to get to San Manuel Chaparron as quickly as possible.

It was the first day of the feria, the time everyone who was born there or who ever lived there at one time or another likes to return to visit with old friends and family. It would be my opportunity to see a lot of my own friends and family. My niece's husband is a colonel in the Guatemalan army. He picked me up at the airport on the morning of my arrival and took me to the military telecommunications base, where he is the base commander. I got the grand tour of the base and had breakfast with some of his staff and a group of young women students who were being honored that day. In the afternoon, we drove to Chaparron, where his five-year-old daughter was being honored as Reina Infantil (honorary pageant princess) of the feria.

Once the feria was over, life in Chaparron returned to normal. As my godson is the mayor, life is easy for me here. I spend a lot of time walking around town, chatting with old friends and family. On my daily strolls, I often encounter people who still remember me from my 1960s Peace Corps days and the projects and activities for this Guatemalan community that occupied my time back then.

A lot has changed in the past 45 years. What were once dusty dirt byways are now carefully paved and groomed roads with plants, decorative statues, benches and fountains. No longer do cattle, burros and mules roam the streets. The old church, the *alcaldia* (municipal government complex) and several homes have been completely rebuilt and modernized. Electrical, telephone and cable TV wires are everywhere. Two large cell phone towers loom over the highest points in town. It seems as though no one walks anymore. There are at least six *tuctucs* (three-wheeled taxis) and vehicles of every description, from heavy trucks to sports cars and even one Cadillac Escalade.

Not everything has changed. National grocery store chains have not yet made their way to Chaparron. I like to stop at the street vendors and buy such things as *jocotes*, *nisperos*, *granadillas* (pomegranates), avocados, *mutas*, papayas and *piñas*. Some of these treats I can get in my native Wisconsin, but many are unheard of back there.

Most of the people here wonder at my enjoyment of *frijoles volteados, chiltepes, queso fresco* and freshly made tortillas almost daily. My sister-in-law made me a dish of *churascos* (grilled beef) with rice and avocado today. As I was struggling, trying to chew the tough stringy meat, I glanced up at my brother-in-law, struggling just as I was, and we both burst out laughing. Where else can you enjoy such flavorful meat, yet have to work so hard just to be able to swallow it?

Young people still walk by on their way to and from school in their traditional uniforms — plaid skirts and white blouses for the girls, dark pants and white shirts for the boys.

This is San Manuel Chaparron. I love it here.

BIKING THE COCONUT SHELL ROAD

(Excerpts from her Travel Journal and an e-mailed letter to Guatemala III.) By Betsy Markland Schwartz

February 24, 2005

I'm about to retire after 25 years of teaching and counseling. March 4 is my last day. I absolutely love my job, but I want more time to be involved in other things. I plan to treat myself to a nice bike ride.

So many kids in my middle school ask why I want to retire. They would just die if they knew that I am 63 years old. They would wonder how I can still ride a bike.

I plan to ride with my good friend Jane (five years my senior!) from the U.S.-Mexico border to Guatemala City, via Copper Canyon and down the Gulf coast.

We will leave the United States in mid-March and hope to arrive in Guatemala in mid-May. We plan to stay there a couple of weeks with my son Chris and his family, then head home by plane.

Jane and I have taken several bike rides together over the last few years — Tunisia, Cuba, Bhutan and Indonesia, to mention a few.

Saturday, April 9, 2005

Hola. We have a layover day today in Actopán, Mexico. We decided the heat and the traffic have given us reason enough to rest for a day or two to reflect on all that's happened.

On Monday, April 3, our original team of four, who had cycled together for a month as far as Guanajuato, separated. My sister Anne and Jane's husband, Billy, drove back to Guadalajara and then flew to California.

That same day, Jane and I continued on our longer journey, beginning our second month's cycling, toward San Miguel de Allende, a distance of about 85 kilometers. We traveled along beautiful rustic roads with hills and small *ranchos* as our views. All was well until we came to the big highway taking us the last 13 kilometers into San Miguel.

We were hot and tired. It was latish in the day and a huge, long hill strewn with big trailer trucks lay in front of us. Jane was terrified and I was not happy. We got off our bikes and walked along a narrow path up a long hill. Suddenly two adorable policemen got out of their pickup truck and began walking towards us.

One policeman asked if I spoke Spanish. *"Si,"* I told him. He asked if I spoke very well. *"Si,"* I told him. Then he said that he and his friend had been following us for a while and were worried about our safety. He politely asked if it would be all right if he gave us a lift up the big hill to the city. When I translated to Jane what they were saying, she jumped for joy and said, "YES!"

The policemen were delighted and so were we. However, when they tried to lift our bicycles into the truck, they looked at us and said, "You have ridden 80 kilometers already today?"

I think they saw all our gray hairs and wondered how on earth we could pedal those heavy bikes over so many hills for such a great distance.

San Miguel was lovely, with all the old historic colonial buildings, its beautiful Gothic-style cathedral waiting to be covered in Saran Wrap by the famous Cristo, and its Spanish restaurant, Rincón Español, which served paella and had a flamenco-dance show.

The next morning we were off to Querétaro, the capital city of the Mexican state by the same name. Querétero is a city of almost a million people. We had read that it is a UNESCO world heritage city because of the street plan. That should have been a clue.

The streets we would be biking over were all cobblestone. And, they were in a disorganized pattern, so that we never knew where we were. But, never mind. I want to share our fun experiences on that day.

We were cycling along, in the heat, with lots of traffic, when all of a sudden, three cyclists came toward us, their bikes loaded to the hilt. It turned out they were cycling from the tip of southern Argentina and heading to the tip of the northern part of Canada.

They were two brothers, and the Bolivian girlfriend of one of them. They had been on the road for well over a year and hoped to finish in September of this year. They appeared to be in their mid-20s.

They were filming and photographing and wanted to bring geography into the classroom. Since this is basically what I just retired from — so many fantastic years of bringing geography and history into the classrooms of Watsonville, CA — I could easily identify with them. They were great to talk to. They were Canadian, so now Canada will also benefit from their travels.

As we approached Querétero City, the traffic snowballed on the four-lane, divided highway. Soon, we lost our shoulder and had nowhere to cycle, except the road, competing with the rush-hour traffic. It was no fun. We barely survived. We found a lovely hotel on the main plaza, and were anxious to leave the city the next morning at 6 a.m. to avoid commuter traffic.

Our decision proved useful only to a point. At 6 a.m. it was still pitch black. Navigating by street lights, we made our way beyond the city where there were no more lights. What could we do? The answer, of course, was to play a few hands of honeymoon bridge, under the last street light, until 7:15, when it was finally light enough to see and be seen as we began climbing a long hill.

I have not mentioned that we were surrounded by towering mountains and were always going up and down between 6,000 and 7,500 feet of altitude, which in itself made the cycling challenging. That, combined with loads that were much too heavy, made our average cycling speed not much more than seven to nine miles per hour.

Wednesday brought us new friends and places of interest. We saw an intriguing building that I thought might be an orphanage. We remembered that in San Miguel we had donated money to students collecting for an orphanage with a name similar to the one we were looking at.

We left our bikes and entered the impressive Casa de Los Angeles. It turned out that it was just a storage area and a shop to sell *artesanías* (crafts), which would be opening soon.

Joaquín, the young welder who lives and works there, was interesting and pleasant. He had spent time working in the States, as most of the people we met there had done at some time in their lives. He had only gone to primary school, but had incredible talent as an artist and welder. He could look at pictures in magazines and weld replicas for his patron. He had a warehouse of beautiful metal and iron objects he had made. Many were sent to a shop in Juárez.

That night we found a wonderful hotel with a pool in Tequisquiapán. It felt so cool to get in that pool and relax all those tired muscles after a long hot day.

It takes us so long to get anywhere because we keep stopping to talk all the time. People pull us over on the sides of the road to talk to us. Where are you coming from? Where are you going? HOW OLD ARE YOU?

Many times those who stop are doing so because they, too, are or were cyclists. It makes for pleasant days, despite the traffic and heat.

Thursday took us to Ixmilquiapán. Don't you love these place names? I am always pronouncing them wrong. I put the accent on the wrong syllable all the time. But, we get there just the same. And, every day there is something remarkable, something to talk about.

This day we started cycling about 9 a.m., after a delicious *huevos rancheros* breakie, and cycled 34 kilometers. We came to a tiny town and decided to find a place to eat our avocados, cheese and bread from the food bag. We had been warned there would not be a restaurant until kilometer 40. Usually we get hungry 30 to 33 kilometers into the ride.

We found a little shop that sold cold drinks and a courtyard around the corner. We were sitting there eating when a well-dressed handsome man came along and started talking to us. He tried to guess our ages. Imagine!

Then he told us that the spot where we were sitting was the courtyard of a factory where all kinds of clothes were made and shipped to other parts of the world, including the United States. We asked if we could visit it. His brother came and walked us through the factory, situated in a gorgeous building built by the Spaniards in the late 1700s.

It was a *hacienda* that had been passed down in the family until someone finally donated it to this tiny town to use as it wanted. The townspeople decided it would become a clothing factory. It may have resembled a sweatshop, except that the workers were pleasant looking and worked with music and air conditioning. They made bras, pajamas, bathrobes and baby clothing. We saw their giant-sized black bras. Jane asked if they made little bras also. The man proudly said yes and asked one of the seamstresses to show us. She brought out a giant grocery bag full of small sizes to show us. I took lots of photos of the shy women sewing.

Another day. Another adventure. It's just great!

The next day, we stopped in the middle of a hill to discuss our options. There was no shoulder on the road, and it was dangerous.

One option was to stop a pickup truck and ask if the driver would take us to the top of the hill. We stuck our arms out at the first vehicle we saw. The driver immediately pulled over, but he misunderstood me and thought I wanted him to drive behind us to protect us from the trucks. So, he said, "*Si, si,*" and started to pull away from us. I yelled at him and he stopped. We both laughed when he understood what I really meant. He helped us lift Pumpkin (Jane's bike) and Peanut (my bike) into his truck and off we went, quickly covering the two more kilometers to the top.

Only 10 kilometers later, I had a flat rear tire. The good news was that we were only footsteps away from a tire repair shop. The bad news was that it was closed, as the owner had gone to special noon mass for the Pope.

We walked farther into town and discovered another tire repairman, who had lived three years in North Carolina and Florida. We had a great discussion while he struggled with my rear wheel. I told him how much I appreciated his help, as the rear tire is always so difficult for me to change. He kept repeating, "I have never seen a bike like this!" Both Jane and I travel on small bikes called Bike Fridays.

We found a little shop where we planned to buy a cold drink and eat our cheese and avocado. There we met Angela and Alfonso, Otomi Indians in their late sixties. The state of Hidalgo has about 300,000 Otomi Indians, and I had very much wanted a chance to talk to some of them. Our new friends owned a small variety shop. They invited us to sit at their table inside, where it was cool, and served us homemade vegetable soup and fresh cheese. As we sat together, we shared our life stories.

They told us they were the last generation to speak their Indian dialect. Their children and grandchildren do not want anything to do with their heritage. One of their sons had gone "al norte," to the States for better work.

I took photos of them and asked for their address, so I could send them one. But they had never received mail before. (Imagine not having to deal with all the junk mail that fills our boxes daily.) Alfonso thought about it for a moment. Then he wrote down seven lines of directions for the mail carrier. To ensure delivery, he wrote the local phone number at the bottom.

As I write all this, it is Saturday and we are resting. It seems everyone in this town knows who we are. This morning a man told us to visit the ruins at Tula, said to be the birthplace of the Aztecs and Quetzalcoatl. Since we are going to Guatemala and will see all kinds of archaeological ruins, he wanted us to see where it all began.

So, we will cycle on for a while, then ride a bus over the biggest mountains.

April 20, 2005

"A trip of 1,000 miles begins with a single step," or in our case, a single pedal.

Muy buenas tardes [A very good afternoon]. At the end of this day, we are 75 miles southeast of Veracruz. We'll have to take a bus at some time to help us get to Palenque by April 29. From Palenque, we will cycle for three days and cross the river to

Guatemala. There, we'll cycle for a couple days and stay overnight in Cobán with Ashley, a former Guatemala III Peace Corps volunteer. We'll cycle for a couple more days and my son Chris will pick us up on the main road into Guatemala City. We'll be there on Mother's Day. And I will see my granddaughter again. Sounds so easy, doesn't it?

We took a bus over the mountains to Papantla, near the east coast, several hundred kilometers north of Veracruz. Papantla is known throughout Mexico as the place of the Voladores, "people who fly" off the tops of high poles. I had seen a photo of them in my Lonely Planet guidebook and was eager to see them perform. We were told that they "fly" daily at noon at the nearby ruins of El Tajín. There the Totonaca civilization flourished from 200 to 600 A.D. The people had built an imposing town with several pyramids, ball courts and other spectacular architectural delights, then abandoned it all. However, the Totonacan descendants still practice the ancient custom of flying as a sun worship event.

At noon tourists gathered at the entrance to El Tajín's ruins and five men appeared, dressed in elaborate bright red pants with headdresses of a fruit basket-like affair and colored streamers wrapped around their necks.

One man played a drum with a flute attached to it, while the other four did a ceremonial dance. One by one, they climbed the notched 30-meter metal pole to a steel platform on the top. While the musician continued to play, the other four, representing the four cardinal directions, each attached themselves to a rope and leaned over backwards and slowly descended, flying around and around the pole as their ropes unwound from the top. It was so smooth and beautiful to watch. They landed upside down, then slowly dropped their feet to turn right side up. It was indeed a spectacular event.

We have had another great week of cycling. Heading south down Mexico's east coast has been beautiful but not easy. We have had to deal with enormous trucks moving very fast on roads with no shoulders. Our worst ordeal is when one gravel truck coming from the opposite direction passes another on our side of the road and leaves absolutely no room for us.

The truck drivers are as courteous as they can be, given their lack of space. Jane and I laughed the other day when we finally got on one of the *autopistas*, Mexico's wide, four-lane roads. It had a shoulder — a safe place for us to ride! We could relax and talk a little. Well, we couldn't actually talk because the roar of the trucks meant the only communication was screaming at each other. That gets really tiring.

When the days are tough, with all the trucks and traffic, we always manage to find a quiet place to sit down for a while, have a cold drink and play a hand of bridge. It is the most relaxing thing we can think of and it helps.

For the most part, it is really not that bad. As we ride, always visible on the other side of the road is the beautiful Gulf of Mexico, with its clear blue-green-colored waters and always a breeze blowing.

We try to find places to stay near the beach, if possible. One day, we had covered the distance that would take us to a hotel near the beach called Bocas Andreas. There are only a few hotels and we never really know what condition they will be in. Usually they are quite nice, clean, and with a restaurant attached; but this time we arrived at the end of the day. We had to stay wherever we could.

From the outside the hotel looked terrible. It was badly in need of paint, and all the wooden frames around the windows were rotted out and filled with termites.

But we had no choice. It would have to be our home for the night. As we stood there, looking up at the grungy old building, a group of scantily-clad teenagers exited the reception room; and at that same time another young man carrying a semi-automatic weapon arrived. He put the gun down, then asked if he could help us with anything. I said we wanted a room.

He took us upstairs to a vacant room, our worst room to date. We were sure there would be bed bugs, and if we hadn't been so tired, we might have tried to cycle to another town. We reluctantly told him we would take it.

But there is a good side to this story. We asked the young man if there was a place to eat nearby. He said everything had already closed at 5:00 p.m., but his mother had a place down the road and if we hurried she might still be there.

We hurried! And she was still there with her husband. They cooked a delicious fish dinner. Because we were so hot and dirty and tired, they said they would cook it and deliver it to us in our hotel room, where we could eat at our leisure, since they were closing. We had room service in our dilapidated, dirty hotel room. And, there were NO bed bugs!

Next morning, we headed to Veracruz's capital, the city of Xalapa [Jalapa]. For years, I have wanted to see the famous Olmec heads — basalt and lava rock carvings measuring up to 2.7 meters, nine feet, more or less, and weighing up to 26 tons. They were made by Mexico's oldest cultural group, the Olmecs, who came mostly from the states of Veracruz and Tabasco. Perhaps they were made to honor the highest-ranking people in their society. Carved as many as 3,000 years ago, they are incredible works of art and truly amazing.

For years, I had a picture of one of these heads on my refrigerator. "Some day, I will get to see these heads," I would say to myself.

In Xalapa's wonderful anthropological museum are seven of the 17 heads known to exist. They were carved between 2000 B.C. and 100 A.D.

The first sighting of the heads was reported in 1878, but until 1945, nothing was done to move them or study them. We will have had the good fortune to see at least 10 to 12 of the possible 17, now scattered around these two southern states.

Each one is different, with some sort of headdress that appears to compress the head, making them rather odd-looking. One shows teeth and another, delicate features, which they think represented a woman.

We found one in the bus terminal the other day and another at the entrance to the City of Veracruz. We are now cycling to Santiago Tuxtla, where I have been told we will find another one.

We hope we can find the one with its eyes closed and mouth open, which represents death, and we think we know the town where to find it.

For now, Jane is patiently waiting. We must look at the map again and see if we can find an option, other than crossing that gigantic towering bridge tomorrow morning.

April 22, 2005

¡Saludos a todos! [Greetings to all!] Here comes the answer I know all of you are waiting for. Did we get across the giant bridge? Well, this is what happened.

I worried much of the night about the metal section of that humongous bridge. I kept thinking of another bridge-crossing experience, when I traveled across the States by bike. The most difficult thing was crossing the steel bridge over the Mississippi River.

But things seem to work themselves out on most of my trips and this story, too, has a wonderful ending.

It turned out the bridge was under repair, closed off on one side. All cars, trucks and buses had to use just one lane at a time. We got to the entrance of the bridge and saw what was happening. When our lane stopped, we asked the construction worker in charge of the traffic if we could go to the front of the line. He said yes and started us off immediately. We proudly rode two abreast so that no vehicle could pass us. Everyone had to go at the pace of the two older women on bikes — up, up and over my dreaded, terrifying bridge, which actually turned out to be asphalted and was just fine.

Once again in my life, I had to just "walk (bike) through my fear." And once again it worked.

April 28, 2005

Was it Odysseus, or Betsy, who was given the great challenges?

More than a week ago, we had to push our heavily loaded bikes over a six-kilometer stretch of sand-covered cobblestone road. Then came the bridge challenge. Now I must tell you about our latest adventure. Let me preface the story by saying that the temperature here in the southern part of Mexico is about 105 degrees with 96 percent humidity.

To make it through our usual 10-hour day is enough of a challenge. But, three days ago, we had a little more to deal with. I had selected a small yellow road on the map. Yellow indicates less traffic and more local interest along the way, so we love to take those roads whenever possible.

I had inquired from the locals about a 30-kilometer section of our planned 80-kilometer day, because that section of yellow line on the map was very thin. Several people said there were problems in different areas, but we probably would be able to get through on bikes.

We realized we might have to push our bikes for a while, but that was okay. We've done that before. We were willing to take that remote road along the coastline.

What we didn't realize was that several years ago severe storms had washed away many sections of the road, which is no farther than one football field's length from the Gulf of Mexico. Even though petroleum has been discovered all over the state of Tabasco, and access for petroleum trucks is essential, the road has never been adequately repaired.

People in that area had taken it upon themselves to repair the destroyed road by building a path through the jungle, parallel to the washed out road. They tossed the branches of coconut palm trees and coconut shells on top of the sand. That was the new path for vehicles.

Since they got no financial help from the government or the oil company, they charged every vehicle 10 pesos ($1) to pass over the stretch they had "repaired." That worked for 4 x 4s, trucks and many cars.

It does not work for bicycles. Have you ever tried to ride a fully loaded touring bike over a coconut shell road built over deep sand?

Well, don't!

Jane and I had to push Pumpkin and Peanut in the hot sun, over the sand-and-coconut-shell road.

It took forever!

Only once did anybody have the nerve to ask the two struggling, not-so-young women to pay the 10 pesos fee. And we wouldn't pay! We took a route over the sand dunes instead, and struggled a little harder. At times, I couldn't believe we were in Mexico. It looked so much like a section of Mongolia's Gobi Desert where my sister and I visited a couple of years earlier.

After finally completing that 30-kilometer section, we stopped for cold water and cheese *quesadillas*. We were so happy to hear the man give us the good news that "from here on to Paraíso, the road is paved."

The cycling was, as I have already pointed out, challenging. Either the weather or the road conditions, or both at once, almost always made it so. The people along the way, however, continued to be courteous and tried to protect us in any way they could.

Stopping for breakfast the other morning, I got out the money to pay, and the señora said, "No, I don't want your money. It was just so nice talking with you two. Go well on your journey."

Now we have entered the region of the classic Mayan culture. We will be passing through it for the rest of our journey to Guatemala. We have jumped to the time period of 100-to-900 A.D. and have just finished one entire day of marveling at the ruins of

Palenque, which were featured in an issue of <u>National Geographic</u> back in 1997. The ruler, Pacal, his son and grandson made this the finest example of a "stone city in the jungle."

Our day-trip to the ancient ruins started with us climbing to the top of the pyramid called the Temple of the Inscriptions (so named because of the great number of recently deciphered glyphs found there) and ended with us descending about 100 slippery stone steps into the death tomb of Pacal.

Not everyone can go into the tomb. Great effort is being made to protect the site, and only a few visitors a day are permitted. To obtain permission, you must write a full-page essay explaining why you want to go.

I did that, and we were accepted. We were given a 20-minute time slot for the viewing. It was extraordinarily exciting, much like seeing King Tut's tomb in Egypt.

Tomorrow morning, very early, we move onward. We really don't know what lies ahead. Howler monkeys, snakes, mosquitos, butterflies? The map just shows a road — a red line this time — straight through most of the jungle of Chiapas.

Will we find lodging in the jungle or have to use Jane's emergency tent? Will we find food and water along the way? And what happens when we cross the Usumacinta River and enter Guatemala, the country I first came to know and love as a Peace Corps volunteer? I served there from January 1964 until August 1965. It is where my son, Chris, was born and now lives with his wife and my granddaughter. I can't wait to see her.

We have been told that the road from Bethel, on the Guatemalan border, is not paved. So, for the next 80 kilometers, we will be on gravel. Can we possibly push Pumpkin and Peanut 80 kilometers to Sayaxché, where the new paved road starts?

Stay tuned for my final edition of "Travels with Betsy," coming out after May 10, as we are scheduled to meet Chris and the TV cameras on May 9. Meanwhile, I'll keep writing as often as I can. Please wish us a little luck on our last section of this wonderful journey.

May 5, 2005

Guess where I am? At the internet café in Cobán, Guatemala. Jane and I rolled in here (well, actually, we weren't rolling too well, because I had a flat tire) two days ago.

We have been staying in Ashley's and Marcio's fantastic stone house, eight kilometers out in the valley of San Juan Chamelco. It was wonderful to see our fellow Guatemala III Peace Corps volunteer again after 40 years. She has spent all of those years here in Guatemala. She looks wonderful.

Ashley and Marcio are busy doing a million things, mostly with their hostel and restaurant, which has the best food in Guatemala. Her homemade cookies and the macadamia nuts they grow are the best. I don't know how they fit in time to host us, but they sure did a great job of it.

At 4:30 this morning, they sent us off on a bus to a national park. The nearby nature reserve opened in 1976, where the famous quetzal birds, almost 800 of them, now live. We wanted to see if we could spot one. The quetzal is Guatemala's national emblem, as we Guatemala III's all remember. It symbolizes freedom.

At 6 a.m. we spotted our first quetzal, just as we were stepping off our bus. There, on the branch of a *guarumo* tree, two meters above my head, sat a beautiful female. Her bright red breast was dramatic against her emerald-green feathers.

When I whispered to Jane, the quetzal flew off. After 30 minutes of waiting for her return, we saw a male quetzal, with his two-foot-long green tail feathers shimmering in the early morning sunlight.

Historically, male quetzal feathers were used by the Mayans and Aztecs to make headdresses. The birds were captured and then released after their tail feathers were removed. In the next molting season, they would grow new tail feathers.

In real life the tail is much more beautiful than in any photograph. There is absolutely no substitute for seeing something with one's own eyes. I guess that is why I travel so much.

Unfortunately, I did not capture the quetzals on film. But I surely captured them in my heart and memory forever.

I always thought the quetzal was extinct or nearly so when I lived here as a Peace Corps volunteer in the 1960s. Didn't you all? Has anyone else, other than Ashley, ever seen a quetzal in the wild? Seeing those magnificent birds was perhaps the biggest surprise of our whole journey.

I want you all to know how exciting it was to get here to Cobán. Being able to stop at Ashley's — another Guate III Peace Corps mini-reunion — added another dimension to the trip. Tomorrow we leave to cycle the last two days of our trip, and then we'll see Chris, Brenda and Nikki. Chris said he's coming to meet us at El Rancho with the TV people. That's all I know.

May 10, 2005 (Mother's Day)

We DID it! We DID it! We DID it!

Our two-month bicycle ride from the U.S. border through Mexico to Guatemala City is finished. We are celebrating Mother's Day with my son and his family in Guatemala City.

Looking back, the biggest disappointment came during that long straight red line on the map leading through the jungle of Chiapas, across the river and over the hills to Guatemala. It was full of surprises, some wonderful, some not so great.

What I thought was going to be rainforest and jungle with tropical birds, monkeys and snakes turned out to be mostly small cattle farms and cornfields. For some time now, apparently, settlers have been cutting down the rainforest, burning the underbrush and starting cattle farms or planting fields of corn.

For 10 days, we cycled in areas with such heavy smoke in the distance that at times we could feel it in our lungs and eyes. Other times we cycled through areas that were still burning.

Both the governments of Mexico and Guatemala know what is happening, but the situation is hard to control, especially since no other work can be found for these poor settlers.

At times, I felt like sitting on the side of the road and crying. Look what is happening to our earth. And we do nothing to stop it.

We found small villages and lots of houses along the whole stretch of road leading us to the Usumacinta River. The villages provided us with all the water and food we needed for 150 kilometers.

Before we started on the recently paved highway, a travel company in Palenque assured us there would be a lovely restaurant about halfway that likely would have cabañas we could sleep in.

Willi Fonseca's Valle Escondido Restaurant was like a slice of heaven for two weary, hot travelers. New cabañas with two rooms, a private bath and a large ceiling fan were more than we ever hoped for.

Our fish and vegetable dinner was topped only by the fantastic buffet breakfast of fresh fruits, eggs, bacon, beans, tortillas and juices. It was certainly a welcome surprise to find this modern and comfortable accommodation our first night in the "big bad jungle."

The following oppressively hot day took us 75 kilometers farther on the road to the ruins of Bonampak (meaning painted walls in Yucatecan Mayan). Arriving 45 minutes before closing gave us little time to enjoy the famous frescoes.

Bonampak is a small Mayan ruin with a main plaza where a large pyramid sits. About 20 meters up the steps of the pyramid are three small rooms, each covered in frescoes. It is for these frescoes that the site is named. Each room features beautifully preserved paintings of either musicians dancing, prisoners of war being tortured by ripping off their fingernails, or bloodletting as a way to get in touch with ancestors. Some archeologists believe all three motifs were part of the ceremony honoring the new heir to the throne. The frescoes were made in the late 700s A.D.

The next day we arrived at the Frontera Corozal early enough in the day to cross the Usumacinta River and sail for 35 minutes on a long, narrow, wooden boat east to the Guatemalan border at a tiny town called Bethel.

The boatman kindly helped Jane and me carry our heavy bikes up a steep sandy embankment and walked us to the immigration office. It was

Sunday and the Mexican immigration office was closed, so we had to leave Mexico without getting our passports stamped. However, the Guatemalan office was open.

The boatman left us in front of the Bethel entry spot, the drunken immigration officer welcomed us into Guatemala, and then proceeded to give us specific instructions on why we must NOT go on our bikes into Guatemala City. He said Guatemala is a very dangerous place and has lots of gangs, robbers and thieves. He relaxed a bit when I told him we would not be cycling in the city, as my son would meet us on the main road before we got there.

The next 80 kilometers were over a rock and dirt road, so we found a mini-bus to take us. Poor Pumpkin and Peanut were thrown on top and tied to the roof rack, while the driver stuffed over 20 people into a 12-passenger van. We bounced and swayed for two hours as we sped to the paved road.

Once on the new highway, we had only 13 kilometers to pedal to the ferry, which took us across the Río Pasión to the town of Sayaxché in Guatemala's most remote department, El Petén.

We took a much deserved layover day in Sayaxché to enjoy a river trip to the seldom-visited Mayan ruins at El Ceibal. A national park has been built there and our guide and boatman, Lázaro, after leading us up a long staircase of primitive stone steps, allowed us to experience the wonders of the rain forest. He pointed out howler monkeys, parrots, toucans and kingfishers, as well as long trails of large ants.

Sadly, at the same time, the fires that we have continued to find everywhere are approaching this national park and the army has just been called in to dig trenches around the perimeter to protect the park.

All along our route, we have been amazed to find so many people, shops and hotels. The people we spoke with were just as amazed at us for daring to take a bike ride along this hot, humid and notoriously dangerous route. There were always three questions: Where are you coming from? Where are you going? How old are you?

It is always fun to hear the people gasp when we tell them our ages. They are proud of us and always wish us a safe journey. I do enjoy seeing how so many people can celebrate others' successes.

From Sayaxché, we worked hard, as I was eager to arrive at the city of Cobán, a couple of hundred kilometers away. From Cobán, we thought we had only to descend 4,000 feet over the next 150 kilometers. We allowed a couple of days to do it. But we quickly learned that it would not be a descent until the second day. The first day was all rolling hills that took us higher and higher into the mountains.

The temperature was more pleasant at higher altitudes. We found a lovely place to sleep, and enjoyed delicious soups, salads and vegetable dishes. There has not been a shortage of food anywhere on this trip.

Our last day of cycling was one of descending steep hills on curvy roads. However, the road had just been repaved and had a shoulder good for bicyclists and pedestrians. The best news of all was its light traffic.

I like speed. Jane does not. We resolved this difference to our mutual satisfaction. I would speed down the hill a short distance and then stop and wait. Jane would get there, and I would take off again. And down, down, down we went.

That day, we had a plan to meet my son, Chris, between 2:00 and 3:00 p.m. at Sarita's Restaurant at the end of the road, where it intersects with the main road coming from Guatemala City. I was on an all-time high. I would reach my goal of cycling to my son's house in time for Mother's Day.

At the same time, I was sad that a wonderful cycling journey with my close friend Jane was coming to an end.

At 1:35 p.m., a blue Toyota pickup sped up the hill toward us. As it approached, the driver leaned out the window and yelled, "Hey, Betsy and Jane!" and then was gone.

I picked up the pace, knowing the driver would be back as soon as he found a safe place to turn around. Chris caught up and stopped in front of us. All of us embraced and started jabbering away.

When Chris asked, "Do you want to put your bikes in the truck?" I had to say, "no." We really wanted to finish the last 17 kilometers by bike and meet him at Sarita's as planned. It is reported they have excellent ice cream.

Chris kindly agreed, asked for my camera and took some fun shots of us cycling over our last stretch as he followed along behind us.

The rainy season, which traditionally starts in May, opened just as we were all seated in the truck and driving home to Guatemala City. Thunder, lightning and driving rain pounded us, making the trip longer than expected. Jane and I marveled at how lucky we were to have finished the entire ride without any rain.

Brenda and eight-month-old Nikki were waiting for us as we entered the lovely home of my son and his family.

We had arrived in Guatemala just as we had planned, on the eve of Mother's Day.

We spent the day with a reporter from the daily newspaper, La Prensa Libre. She hoped to publish the story either the following Sunday or the next. Her interview was followed by another, with a reporter and cameraman for Quatevisión, a local TV station, which will have a short clip on the news sometime this weekend.

We have been busy from the moment of arrival, but not too busy to celebrate a memorable Mother's Day with Chris, Brenda and Nikki.

It is hard to believe that our cycling is over for this trip. Yes, it had difficult moments, but all in all, we took it slowly and worked our way through the heat, the hills, the bad roads and the bridges. We averaged no more than 50 to 70 kilometers each day, making a total of 1,653 kilometers, a little over 1,000 miles cycled.

What sticks with me most are the marvelous moments with the people we met, the sights we saw, the geography of the land we passed through, and all that we learned about the Olmecs, the Toltecs and the Mayans. Rolling over the land, feeling its every bump, helped us better visualize what life may have been like for those people so many centuries ago.

It's all part of the wonders of a bicycle trip, in which you travel at a slow pace and have time to think about what you have seen.

It was a great trip and I am so happy to be here now, spending time with my granddaughter and watching her grow. Today we accompanied Nikki and her mama to Nikki's first class at the baby gym. When she came home, she crawled for the first time.

And I was there to see it!

MY OLD NEIGHBORHOOD

By Betsy Markland Schwartz

Hi all. I am here in Guatemala visiting my son, Chris, his wife Brenda, and their family. Below is a short account of my experiences here yesterday:

Today was an emotional high for me as I stepped back 47 years to find the *aldea* (village) where I lived and worked as a Peace Corps volunteer. My daughter-in-law's dad, Luis, offered to drive me there. He once worked in that area and thought he knew how to get there. So off we went to find the small *aldea* outside Guatemala City.

We finally located the town and the church that had been at the center of much of Mike's and my work as Peace Corps community developers back in the 1960s. The church, which once had only a dirt path leading to it and a small school next door, appears much bigger now and well-preserved.

We searched for the house that Mike and I had lived in, the house that our son Chris had lived in for the first nine months of his life. Everything was so different and more modern than the little mud houses where most of the indigenous population had once lived.

In a cantina, I told an old gray-haired woman that I was looking for Cristina, who was 14 years old back when I was a volunteer. The woman gave us directions to Cristina's house.

Luis drove there, we knocked on a big garage door, and a young boy opened it. When I asked if Cristina lived there, he said yes. I pushed right by him and walked to the open door of a room where a woman was sitting, reading. She looked up and stared at me for about five seconds, then broke into a wide smile, leaped up and said, "¡DOÑA BETSY!" Oh, how we laughed and cried!

Cristina brought me up to date on most of my friends from so long ago. Some have died, many have lived to a very old age. One man, Don Meme, had died only three years earlier at the age of 98.

Cristina walked with me to my old house. We knocked on the door and the woman living there let us come in. We sat on the back porch and shared stories. The place sure looked different 47 years ago. The current owner has planted a lot of trees and has many dogs and small sheds. Only the *pila* (a place to wash clothes) remained the same. It is where Cristina helped me so much, for when she was a teenager I hired her to wash baby Chris's diapers.

I also discovered the origin of the name "Lo De Bran." Both Cristina's family and the family now living in my former house have the last name Bran. They were part of a large family, whose members owned a large parcel of land. Hence the name of the *aldea*.

We visited another friend of mine, Martina, who had been only a child when I lived there. She still lives the life of a farm woman, keeping her five cows in front of her house. She has a hired-man who finds and cuts fresh grass every day for the cows she keeps for selling milk.

For some, life remains much the same, despite the dramatic outward changes in this once small agricultural village that had no water or electricity 47 years ago.

Cristina told me that on the day of my visit she had been planning to go with one of her daughters to San Cristóbal to help with the therapy for two of her grandchildren. But at the last minute she had decided she didn't want to go. She stayed home and I walked in her door.

One never knows what a day will bring!

WHY I CELEBRATE PEACE CORPS

By Lynda Sanderford Morrison

On the 47th anniversary of the Peace Corps, I was seated in the auditorium of the U.S. embassy in Yerevan, Armenia. The building had once been the headquarters of the communist youth league in the former Soviet Union. As the U.S.S.R weakened in the early 1990s, Armenia declared its independence, and the empire disintegrated further. The U.S. was the first country to recognize Armenian independence, and soon afterward the new nation requested Peace Corps volunteers to serve there.

These volunteers now sat around me, my husband, and my son. The Peace Corps director and U.S. Ambassador Lemon opened the ceremonies. At one point, all those who were serving and had served in the Peace Corps were asked to stand, state their name, country and years of service. When the roll call reached us, my husband rose and in his booming voice said, "Gordon Morrison, Iran IV, 1964 to 1966." I followed, "Lynda Sanderford Morrison, Guatemala III, 1963 to 1965." Our son stood and continued, "Gregory Morrison, Morocco, 1995 to 1996." The audience, impressed with so many Morrisons, had a laugh when the next young man also added Morrison to his name.

The moment spoke to me of how important the Peace Corps had been in our lives. Greg was then a Foreign Service officer on his first overseas appointment for the Department of State. Gordon and I had met when we became Peace Corps training officers in 1966 for a group to be sent to Micronesia. My choice of studies in Latin American history was directly related to my Peace Corps experience in Guatemala. In so many ways, we were truly a Peace Corps family.

When Senator Ted Kennedy and his niece Caroline took the stage with Barack Obama on Jan. 28, 2008, at the 40th anniversary, I was reminded of the rhetoric that had inspired Gordon and me to go out and "do something for your country." I chose to do that something in Latin America because my roommate and best friend was Cuban. She had arrived at my university in 1960, just ahead of the broken relations between Cuba under Castro and the United States. Suddenly, she was a refugee, and I became personally involved in her situation. After graduation, I went off to Peace Corps training in New Mexico learning some Spanish, history, and pointers on how to be a community organizer. John F. Kennedy's assassination during that period only made we trainees more determined to contribute in some way.

I don't know how much of what I did as a Peace Corps volunteer had a lasting effect on Guatemala, but my experience had a lasting effect on me. At the end of my service, I recruited for the Peace Corps on university and college campuses for a year. In 1966, the war in Vietnam had not yet stirred the passion among students that it soon would, but civil rights were a hot topic. My recruiting team ran into racist reactions at a Louisiana restaurant because of our associations with black students, and it reminded us how far we had yet to go to become a color-blind nation.

After I returned home to North Carolina, the Peace Corps contacted me again. They were seeking trainers for a big program in Micronesia. Lyndon Johnson's War on Poverty and Great Society had reached our far-flung United Nations trust territories in the Pacific. Micronesians were requesting more development aid and attention. Johnson decided to send hundreds of volunteers as teachers and community workers. Dozens of Micronesians were plucked from their islands to help with the training. Corporate executives, returned volunteers, Micronesians, linguists, psychologists, and caterers gathered at a once-posh hotel in Key West, Fla.

During the next three months, we created a unique community, a social and cultural milieu with its own set of accomplishments and failures, problems, and conflicts. We experienced romances, spousal abuse, depression to the point of a death, civil rights demonstrations, a Coast Guard rescue, bizarre sexual behavior, and a hurricane. Meanwhile, the linguists and Micronesians hammered out lessons on learning languages that never had been written down. I can only hope this training adequately prepared those who endured it to the end for their next two years. It certainly widened my world even further and helped me to find my life's partner.

Gordon and I married after training and put our skills, honed by Peace Corps service, to work in the coal camps of western Virginia. When the coal companies released their ownership and control over their mining communities at mid-century, the people who remained bought their homes in the mountain hollows but found that company stores, schools, and community centers were boarded up. Since the Methodist Church was often the only institution still present and operating in the camps, its leadership felt an obligation to help improve the lives of the residents. Local ministers, however, usually had little expertise in community development. We were asked to help. Gordon and I moved into a house in the "holler" and did our best to organize activities and introduce a new view of the wider world to our neighbors. Gordon also preached at four churches each Sunday. I imagine many saw us as aliens who spoke of places beyond their experience, but they treated us kindly. We learned about hexes, snake-handling and family feuds. Our stay was too short to do more than organize some committees, get the bookmobile to visit regularly, and have a few educational events. In many ways, our "holler" was as much of a challenge as our service overseas.

Our goal was to return to Iran. Gordon had been corresponding with the Episcopal bishop in Isfahan and with the American Episcopal Church, seeking appointments for us as lay missionaries. Bishop Dehqani was a Muslim convert, a rarity, and our fellow missionaries were mostly British and other Europeans. Isfahan had a large number of Armenian Christians as well. Gordon had already become a member of the community when he was a Peace Corps volunteer. At the university, I had an Iranian roommate for a few months and I looked forward to renewing our friendship. Her family would become an important part of our life, although she lived in the far north of the country. Knowing about the Peace Corps through me, she became the virtual "house mother" of local volunteers.

For Gordon and me, our three years in Iran became a defining experience for our marriage and our continuing interest in the Middle East. Our son, Greg, was born during this time. Gordon helped to establish a new Christian high school and Diocesan youth camps. I attempted to improve the laboratory procedures at the Christian hospital. All the service institutions of the Episcopal Church, however, would be seized during the revolution so this work did not endure. It was the dozens of personal relationships that would survive into the future. Our community would be scattered, some would be arrested and others would die during the revolution that followed our departure. An attempt to bring charges against the bishop failed, so assassins were sent to his home to remove him by other means. Miraculously, he survived the attack and went into exile. His talented son was not so fortunate. Bahram was executed on his way to work. The priest who baptized our son, also a convert from Islam, was martyred in his church one evening. Some of the bishop's staff were arrested. Terry Waite helped secure their release before he too became a hostage in Lebanon.

These events inspired Gordon to once again consider ordination to the priesthood, as he had in earlier years. With another child now, we changed location and focus to allow Gordon to attend the seminary.

Afterward, we decided that the Deep South was where we might best serve. Our path eventually led to Selma, Alabama, where race relations still impacted the lives of its residents to a great degree. The old political tensions endured, although a majority of citizens, we believed, wanted to develop better relations. We were pleased to learn that the public schools had improved so that our son, Christopher, could attend Selma High School rather than a segregated private academy. Gordon regularly met with other clergy and citizens seeking common goals of good education, improved healthcare, and better relations in general. The old political establishment, both black and white, did not seem ready for change, however, except on their own terms. The politics of confrontation prevailed. When the school board fired the black superintendent, demonstrations erupted. The high school was occupied by students and closed down. The national press and the National Guard arrived in town. Because tensions ran so high and the situation was so unpredictable, we felt we had to send our son to a school out of state. The community had taken one step forward and two steps back. We were dismayed but stayed on while I earned my Ph.D. Sadly, the community did not seem able to regain the momentum lost in that interlude of renewed confrontation.

In more recent years, our goal as a family has been to promote better understanding of the cultures we have lived among, especially Christian-Muslim relations. Immediately after the 9/11 attacks, Gordon went to the nearest mosque in Evansville, Indiana, to offer sanctuary to those who felt the need for it. He gave lectures on Islam throughout the community, and I added a class on the Middle East to my teaching schedule at the University of Southern Indiana. On a grant, Gordon and I traveled around the world to study the interface of religions where that contact has been, to date, peaceful or violent. In January, 2009, Gordon returned to Damascus for further discussions with religious leaders and others.

We believe in person-to-person contacts, inasmuch as understanding begins to occur when we meet each other as equals. By joining the Peace Corps, we each became immersed in cultures not our own, and this was the benefit of the experience. It made us think more deeply about our own values and to appreciate those of others. Many of us tried to go out and do something for our country and a hurting world, but we volunteers gained so much more. That is why I gratefully celebrate the creation of the Peace Corps 50 years ago.

PATTERNING PEACE, PIECE BY PIECE

By Bryce Hamilton

As if by some master design, all the pieces of my life seem to have fallen into place simply by my being in the right place at the right time.

That's how it was with the Peace Corps. Time and place perfectly coincided so I would cross paths with Margaret Beshore, and that has made all the difference. I often forget the names of neighbors down the street, but I still remember that dynamic campus recruiter who convinced me to become a Peace Corps volunteer.

Her energy, spirit and challenge changed my life. Had I not met her, I likely would have continued pursuing my goal of a corporate marketing career. I've often wondered what type of lifestyle and world view I would have assumed had I gone down that path.

As it turned out, my two years in Guatemala provided the time and experiences I needed to get to know myself. I loved the independence and variety of my Peace Corps "job." I decided that upon returning to the States I would: 1) explore different kinds of work options, and 2) if possible, run my own business. I've been fortunate. I have achieved both goals.

After the Peace Corps I had a job (along with fellow Guatemala III Peace Corpsman Tim Kraft) at the 1968 Mexico Olympics, and later I worked on the staff of a hunger-education project.

While living in Washington, D.C., I read that Senator Gaylord Nelson of Wisconsin was looking to sponsor a national event called "Environmental Teach-In." I called his office and talked with Denis Hayes, who had been hired to pull it all together. In a very short time, a half dozen of us were working out of an office near Dupont Circle.

We divided responsibilities and I think mine was the "plum" position: encouraging the participation of kindergarten through grade-12 students across the United States. I still have a file of the more moving letters that kids wrote to our office.

During the planning stages, we changed the name to Earth Day, with the hope it would become an annual event. That has happened. Lots of public and private environmental initiatives trace their origins back to that first national observance. We are thinking green now, but there is so much more to be done, especially with lifestyle issues.

In 1972, while living in Denver, my wife and I were again in the right place — this time, a garage sale.

We purchased two antique patchwork quilts, a transaction that changed our lives in ways we never could have dreamed.

Within months we were on the road, living out of a Volkswagen camper and buying and selling quilts across the country. One state at a time, we placed want ads in small-town weekly newspapers and marketed our discoveries through sales sponsored by quilt and antique shops from coast to-coast.

Our timing as gypsies couldn't have been better. Due to the heightened interest in all "Americana" for our country's bicentennial celebration, the United States Information Service sponsored us on a 1976 European tour. Traveling with mounted displays of quilts from our personal collection, we gave lectures and workshops in Iceland, Norway, Sweden, Germany, Romania, Switzerland and England.

When we returned home after that unforgettable year, it was finally time to settle down. We chose to live in Minneapolis.

In 1977, we initiated our own business working with Amish women from whom we had purchased antique quilts. Relying on their sewing skills to make new quilts in queen and king sizes, we continue to provide patterns and fabrics for them to create the handmade quilts that we design and market. Our quilts are sold through selected quilt and specialty shops and at several large annual quilt events. In addition, we own a fabric Christmas ornament business.

I am honored to have gotten to know Amish people, some now for more than 30 years. Their honesty and warmth, quiet and unassuming ways, connection to the natural world and their sense of community have been a beacon of both hope and challenge to my busy and fast-paced urban life.

A memorable event for us every spring is our annual trip to northern Ohio, where the majority of the women we work with live. There, for two or three days, with my car radio turned off, I drive the winding roads and visit my friends, often with a déjà vu Peace Corps feeling as young children gather about and stare, speaking only their German dialect.

One of the advantages of our quilt business is that I don't have to retire. I can just do less and less of it. I still love coming to the studio each day, excited to open the boxes that arrive, and then choosing fabric to send back to the quilters. In every sense, I've had a very fulfilling life.

Over the years, however, Guatemala has never let go of me. The thick corn tortillas, Gallo beer, diesel fumes and jammed "chicken buses," terraced mountainsides, *huipiles* [blouses], *bougainvillea* and *marimbas*. More than anything, memories have drawn me to travel back many times.

I usually travel alone, with just a rucksack, becoming once again, for a short time, a 22-year-old. On each trip I visit a new area of the country. And I always spend a couple of days in Mataquescuintla. I check in at the hotel, and then seat myself on a bench outside the mayor's office.

Word spreads that I'm in town. People who knew my Peace Corps site co-workers Nola Alberts, Marcia Lang and me soon start stopping by to chat. We dust off 40-year-old memories: my inability to handle *aguardiente* [spirituous liquor], Nola's basketball team, our failed jelly-making cooperative, Marcia's helicopter rescue (stories we'll save for our next book), and on-and-on. Those conversations alone make my return trips worthwhile.

In the mid-'80s, I added Nicaragua to my Central American travel schedule. Because of our country's involvement in the Sandanista/Contra conflict, a friend and I founded a people-to-people organization called Project Minnesota-Leon. PML's primary goal, then and now, has been to acquaint Minnesotans with the reality of life in Nicaragua. In many respects, the organization is a grassroots mini-Peace Corps.

PML is advised by a Leon council of citizens and directed by a group of in-country Minnesota volunteers (a number of whom, by the way, have returned from their assignments with Nicaraguan spouses). Efforts have ranged from equipping the Leon municipal band with used musical instruments and helping establish a youth art school to facilitating a program that connects physician-assistant college students with Leon's hospital.

Of all PML's activities, the most gratifying have been the life-changing experiences ot hundreds of Minnesotans who have gone on 10-day delegations arranged by our volunteer coordinator, with each participant living with a low-income Nicaraguan family. One of the first participants in this program, a high school sophomore at the time, is now a professor of Latin American politics at Macalester College.

A connective thread of 40-some years ties me to Guatemala and another thread of 20 years to Nicaragua. A third thread is much more recent. It is the reunions that have reconnected my fellow Guatemala III returned Peace Corps volunteers.

Our two reunions — one in New Jersey in 2003 and one in Guatemala in 2005 — were wonderful in that our common bond and history enabled us to "hit the ground running" as we shared in each other's life journeys.

Even the first reunion felt as if it had been only months since we had last seen each other, certainly not 40 years.

I hope there will be more. These are "family" reunions without the baggage, only camaraderie and joy.

¡Hasta pronto, compañeros!

LIVING IN INDIA, TEACHING COMMITMENT TO A WORLD
WHERE WE LIVE IN PEACE AND HARMONY

By Bob Hetzel

I returned home from my Peace Corps service and became a middle school math and science teacher, teaching at the University of Wisconsin-Milwaukee lab school from 1965 through 1967. At the same time, I was a teacher-trainer with the National Teacher Corps. From 1967 to 1969, I attended the University of Wisconsin-Madison and earned my Ph. D. in educational leadership.

I headed west then, spending the next 20 years as an administrator in Arizona schools. Along the way I became a principal and then a superintendent.

I got the urge to go abroad again in 1994 and served as the superintendent of Cairo American College in Cairo, Egypt. I loved the work, the people, and the life; but I was getting older. So after five years I took my present position as director of the American Embassy School in New Delhi, India.

I love walking onto our campus each day. We serve kids from 52 nations, kids who work, play, argue and complain together. Skin color, house of worship, or passport are not criteria these kids use to judge people. It is so very hopeful to interact with them and their families each day, knowing that this is the way the world can be.

India has great food. India is exotic, chaotic, and exciting. How can you not love the mystique of India? How can you not love a holy cow?

I am now on a quest to be the oldest practicing school administrator in the world and my competition is a 99-year-old monk in Tibet, but I'm gaining on him.

What excites me is that our American Embassy School has adopted a compelling vision. AES is committed to preparing young people for leadership and advocacy in the creation of a world where we live in peace and harmony with one another and our environment. This vision came out of a series of community strategic planning sessions. If we can hold the world together for a while longer, help is on the way.

Teachers were my role models for the American Dream when I was growing up in a blue-collar neighborhood. They wore white shirts and ties, and they were college graduates.

The Peace Corps, for me, was adventure and service. It was also a time to make sure that teaching was what I wanted to do. I have never once regretted my chosen profession. I still love it. Without it, no doubt, I would not be in India competing with that monk.

I've just returned from recruiting teachers. I hired several returned Peace Corps volunteers (30-year olds). I love the connection we make when I say, "I was in the Peace Corps too."

THE WAY WE WERE

By Maggie Neal Kent

[Maggie Neal Kent was the wife of Keni Kent, the CARE director serving Guatemala in the early 1960s. She did double duty as official "caretaker" for Peace Corps volunteers then assigned there. Both of the Kents were and are fondly remembered as good friends of Guatemala III.]

Do you remember that Shakespearean play in which Henry was about to go into a critically important battle? He left his tent and walked among his sleeping men, his heart overflowing with love for them. He wanted to know all the intricate details of their lives. He prayed that the next day would bring victory and that no great harm would come to them.

I had the same feelings from 1963 to 1965 — that I was walking among you Guatemala III volunteers, watching all of you sleep, and dream, and get up to go and live another day.

Finally, now, via "The Book," we will be able to walk with you, up and down the streets of your sites, the days at times so quiet, too quiet, and repetitive. And yet something is afoot — not just the volunteers' dreams but the friendly efforts of local host-country boosters — something that kept you going!

Your writings confirm what I always thought (those long, quiet days and the links with your neighbors, the character and nature of their customs and habits, the unpredictable events), that your stay in Guatemala was at times dreadful and many times revelatory.

You were a clever group, with laughs and affection to spare. My eye-opener was watching you grow as a group. It was like watching birds in flight, or fast-swimming fish, or quick-moving sheep.

No, no, no! — Not sheep! You were not adept at forming a line! You were not interested at all in staying in line!

At the beginning, in Las Cruces training, I thought I was much older than you. Now I know I wasn't, not by much.

Once we go overseas to work, and to serve, great change comes over us. It defines us. I observed in other CARE posts that those who came to work, but not necessarily to serve, made little or no improvement at a basic level and spent much time comparing the United States with the host country. They did that automatically. They had little else to do with their minds and resorted to the easiest response. Dutch, French and Europeans of all ages, like you, took flight and wandered across their host country, discovering it.

Your Guatemala III book project is going to be significant. I am proud to have been part of such a company of fine people!

¡HOLA!

By Norma Wilder Benevides

It's August, 2006, and I just got back from 10 days in Mexico. I don't know when I have had more fun!

Fun, fun and more fun! We don't get enough of it. I just want to laugh and have fun the rest of my life, even though I have a responsible job and a serious side, too.

It is so sad to hear in our e-mails about cancer and other problems in our Peace Corps group, and it makes me wonder how much time I have left.

But, meanwhile, I went to Tampico with a friend who is from Mexico. We went to her nephew's wedding, where we literally danced all night —*cumbia, salsa* and *meringue*, my three favorites, learned at the Saturday-night neighborhood get-togethers we had in Zona 5, El Edén, in Guatemala City, my 1960s Peace Corps site.

Every Saturday at 6:00 p.m. the *marimba* would begin playing and the four *gringas*— Mary Hammond, Anne Cartwright, Elva Reeves and I — would start to dance with the neighbors. Men, women, children, grandparents, everyone was there.

When the *marimba* stopped playing, they put on records and we were not allowed to stop dancing for 12 full hours (am I exaggerating?). So we got pretty good.

Dancing at the wedding in Mexico brought back all those memories. We also visited San Miguel de Allende and Taxco and did all the tourist things in the DF [Federal District], including Xochimilco. There 35 members of one family brought food and drink and we sang up and down the canal.

It was fabulous! So, now it's back to reality and back to work, but with great memories and that wonderful Latin beat I so love.

I am ready to be my American self again, for a while anyway.

HOW THE PEACE CORPS CHANGED ONE GRINGA'S MINDSET

By Carolyn Plage

After my Peace Corps experience, my old political views, learned from my conservative family and early associations at New York University, were turned upside down, inside out, and quite the opposite from my views in 1961 and earlier. I went to several meetings of returned Peace Corps volunteers, a group at NYU with leftist views. I became close friends with a returned volunteer from Ecuador who wound up going to Cuba to cut cane. I might have gone too; but I was then employed as a teacher at the New York Institute for the Blind and supporting myself on the private-school teacher's salary. I am a registered Democrat, but often find myself at odds with the foreign policies of both parties. And with recent events I have become quite pessimistic about the chances of humans ever knowing world peace.

Several years after my Peace Corps experience, our government opposed revolution in Nicaragua and I wrote my first letter to a president of the United States:

Dear President Reagan,

I am writing to you in hopes that you will read and consider my thoughts on our United States and Central American relations. This issue particularly concerns me because I was one of those idealistic early 1960s college graduates who joined the Peace Corps hoping to help keep the world free for "democracy." I spent two years in the beautiful but poverty-ridden country of Guatemala and that two years turned my personal political beliefs upside down.

It was those two years of living and working with the struggling people of Guatemala that made me believe it is impossible for presidents, senators, representatives, ambassadors, reporters, etc. to really know the problems of these countries. How can they suggest solutions while they relax in their posh hotel suites or their well-guarded, tiled, roofed, and floored homes behind 10-foot-high walls with muchachas [servants] serving their meals and cleaning their bathrooms for $20 a month? Perhaps you will say I'm still an idealist, but wouldn't we learn more about making a better world if every college grad or maybe high school grad was "drafted" into a type of Peace Corps, to serve in our own country's impoverished areas or abroad in Third World countries? And. Just to push the idealism further, let's abolish the military branches of our own government and make them into international CCCs [Civilian Conservation Corps] or technical assistance peace corps — no guns allowed!

So what about our policies in Central America? Anyone reading anything of the history of our relations with these countries has got to see it is only logical that Nicaragua should fear a U.S. invasion. We have, since the birth of our own nation, acted time after time as if we were endowed by right of our existence to dictate the type of government and leaders these nations should have. We have completely disregarded the differences of our histories and our peoples and presumed what was good for us must necessarily be good for them. I have not been back to Central America but once since my Peace Corps stint and that was in 1966. However, I keep meeting others who have spent time in these countries — Maryknoll brothers and sisters who have lived and worked there for many years, and representatives of *Witness for Peace* (individuals who went to Nicaragua and stayed at least several months and worked with the people in hospitals, cooperative farms, building projects, etc.). Their stories conflict greatly with what our government tells us. How can this be? Having lived in Guatemala City from 1964 to 1965, during a state of siege, I feel that our officials aren't seeing the whole picture from their private cars and fancy limos as they "investigate" the situation.

In Nicaragua, the Sandanistas may be looking like good friends of Russia. But if they are, I believe it can only be because they rightfully feel they cannot trust the United States. We are driving them into the hands of the Russians by refusing to help them in the ways they most need assistance. Instead, we threaten their attempts at developing a free nation — refusing medical aid, trade, scaring them with a huge military build-up in Honduras and flying our planes overhead. In El Salvador we support a government that, based on all I've read and heard from those going there, is far more "evil" than the Sandanistas. I suggest we change our tune completely — offer only assistance in the fields of medicine, education, farming, and industrial technology, and (dare I say it?) birth control, the rhythm method or whatever. Overpopulation is an agreed-upon problem of most Third World countries. No more arms to anybody, and if we really assist them in good faith in all these other areas they won't need to turn to Russia or any other nation for military supplies.

It's about time that on this teeny, tiny planet with our God-given (or god-given) brains, we learn to use them to help one another despite our differences in politics, ideology, religion, or lifestyle. It's about time *we stop talking about how great the good old U.S.A. is and think of how great we might make the world for ALL — free of hunger, sickness, pollution, and war. Why not? Let's start in Central America!*

ENLARGING AND ENRICHING OUR PERSPECTIVES

By Dave Smits

When I was asked to write an essay about the impact of our Peace Corps experience on my life, I was initially as reluctant as I am these days to take my shirt off in public. Such reluctance was curious, however, for I had absolutely no doubt that our Peace Corps service (my wife, Pat, and my newborn daughter, Susie, served with me) was a fundamental shaping influence on my thinking and behavior. But it's tough, and apt to be colossally boring to others, to bare your soul, as this assignment would require if done well. Even though not in politics, I have not made telling the unembellished truth a lifelong habit. Normally a varnished version fits the bill perfectly well. But there would be no place for shadiness in such an essay. Besides, our fellow Peace Corps volunteers, now in their dotage, have knocked around long enough to recognize the unmistakable odor of humbug, though its various manifestations can deceive even the most seasoned observer of the human condition.

The requested essay would be challenging then. But the more I thought about the matter, the more receptive I was to the challenge. Not that my Peace Corps service had been noteworthy for its accomplishments. It most certainly was not! In truth, at the conclusion of our stay in Guatemala there was every reason for me to be humbled by my meager accomplishments. I remained awkward, tongue-tied, and self-conscious when speaking Spanish. Actually, my decision to accept the challenge of tackling the essay was based, at least partly, on my awareness that I'm a better writer than talker. Admittedly, then, I was too taciturn and private to be a first-rate PC volunteer. Fortunately, as usual, Pat's gift of gab and gregariousness helped to compensate for my deficiencies.

There are, of course, as I try to convince my students, the beneficial outcomes of living abroad in the manner of the host-country nationals themselves. The experience gave me a much broader perspective on many critical issues than I had before my PC service. I grew up in a small predominantly Dutch-American and German-American community in northeastern Wisconsin. De Pere, WI, was not actually the end of the earth, but on a clear day the end could easily be seen from the Knights of Columbus Hall on the edge of town. I was actually born in St. Vincent's Hospital on the east side of Green Bay, and my unwavering devotion to the city's fabled professional football team, the good old "Packers," was nurtured fervently from my first breath. Utterly provincial in outlook, I grew up without any awareness that boys and, for that matter, men and women throughout the world were as enthralled by the game that we North Americans call soccer, as I was about football. Latin Americans call their version of the game "futbol," and they are only slightly less devoted to it than to their children.

My boyhood hometown in Wisconsin was not only unaware of the significance of soccer to the rest of the world, it was also predictably devoid of ethnic and cultural diversity. There were, to my knowledge, no Jews, no Hispanic-Americans, no African-Americans, no Asian-Americans, to name only a few of the groups unrepresented. The town's only exotic inhabitants were a Syrian family. They operated a small grocery store on Broadway Avenue where purchases could be made on Sundays.

I confess that at the time of my graduation from high school, I had no idea what a bagel was. And as for lox, I knew we each had one of them on our high school lockers, but it was not until around mid-life that I sampled the thing, with cream cheese, on one of the aforementioned bagels. Nor would I have recognized a tortilla, a *tamale*, an *enchilada*, a *burrito*, a *quesadilla*, or any other example of the Latin-American cuisine that shares the blame for my present corpulence. We had no African-American families in my hometown. When a black woman with whom Pat had become very friendly while we both were later in graduate school talked about making up "chitlins" for a party she was having, I imagined they were some kind of word games for her guests' entertainment. Had I known that the term in question was a reference to a delicacy prepared from hog intestines, my post-PC cosmopolitanism would have been severely tested. There was not a single Chinese restaurant in all of De Pere; and, with the possible exception of Milwaukee, I'd be surprised if there was one in the entire state of Wisconsin. For all I knew, moo goo gai pan could have been a Chinese emperor, a city, a costume, or a custom revered from antiquity. The most exotic new food that I can remember from my boyhood years was pizza, which I thoroughly disliked upon first sampling.

There was near my boyhood hometown one ethnic minority that was both conspicuous and shame-
fully treated. The Oneida Indians, once one of the
nations of the powerful Iroquois Confederation in
upstate New York, had been relocated to a reservation in Northeastern Wisconsin in the mid-nineteenth
century. The Oneidas lived in poverty and degrada-
tion just outside Green Bay. Often on pleasant Sunday
afternoons my father would pile the family into our
old Plymouth and take us for a drive. We sometimes
wound up passing through the Oneida reservation.
I regret having to admit that my parents' remarks
about the living conditions there and the Indians
themselves were never flattering. Before going to
Guatemala with the Peace Corps, the only truly grim
poverty that I had ever seen was on that Indian reservation. Shacks, dogs, ragged and barefoot children,
junked cars and appliances, hopeless people; it was
all so sad.

But even sadder was the way the non-Indians in
my world smugly disdained those tragic victims of U.S.
advancement. The Oneidas were normally vilified as
lazy, dirty, worthless, irresponsible, unwilling to work
and incorrigibly drunken, among lesser faults. Their
impoverished condition won for them the disparage-
ment and contempt of the local pillars of rectitude.

It is truly ironic and so revealing that striking recent
improvements on the reservation have not produced
a corresponding elevation of the Oneidas in the eyes
of their detractors. Pat and I make it a habit to go
back to Green Bay for at least one Packer game at
Lambeau Field each season. The Monday after one
such recent game we drove our rented car across the
Oneida reservation. The transformation there since
my boyhood years was astonishing. The Oneidas now

236

have a gambling casino which has generated unaccustomed wealth for the tribe. Gone are the shacks of yesterday. New homes, mowed lawns, and shoe-wearing children have replaced the less becoming past versions of the same.

But, and this is the most unfortunate and telling lesson of the story, the recent successes of the Oneidas have not produced a corresponding elevation in the eyes of their non-Indian neighbors. The latter, who once reviled the Oneidas for their lack of success in realizing the American Dream, are now quite jealous of them for their prosperity, and condemn the First Americans as "bloodsuckers." Native Americans have surely not found life in the United States to be a bed of roses.

But to get back to the subject of lessons learned from our Peace Corps experiences, one valuable and often-forgotten realization that I came to is that human beings can live quite happily with minimal material possessions. That seldom-appreciated reality is easily overlooked when living in our prosperous and acquisitive society. Pat and I were as happy as two Chester White hogs in a big ol' vat of slop while serving in Guatemala. The truth is that she and I have accumulated more than our fair share of superfluous material possessions since returning to the States. But at this stage of my dotage, I find myself disposed to shed much of the junk I have stock-piled through the years. I now prefer to live a much more minimalist existence stripped of the expensive and distracting gizmos and status symbols that we in the States regard as indispensable.

Unlike our later wavering ostentation, Pat and I lived on the edge of destitution as PCVs. While stationed in Guatemala City, we got by with a two-burner kerosene stove to do all our cooking. When Pat wanted to do some baking, she merely placed a bottomless tin box over the burners, lit them, and baked the bread, cakes, cookies, etc. that we craved. While she and I served in the capital city, we rarely had the use of a PC jeep or any other internal-combustion-engine vehicle. We pedaled our bikes almost everywhere and usually found them to be quite adequate transportation, as well as aids to physical fitness, and a deterrent to the accumulation of bulky gewgaws. When our bikes proved inconvenient or inadequate, we hopped on one of the city's innumerable buses and found an opportunity to interact with regular folks.

So many of us here in the States spend so much of our lives commuting here and there all alone in our automobiles and deprived of human companionship. The experience isolates us, enables us to dehumanize other drivers, and facilitates our routine displays of aggression and incivility. Moreover, I suspect that our Guatemalan bus trips may have helped disabuse the host-country nationals of the prevailing misperception of people throughout the Third World that North Americans are all filthy rich, pampered, and patronizing.

While Pat and I were living in the mountain village of Comalapa, we had no refrigerator, no TV set, no telephone, no flush toilet, and of course, nothing even remotely resembling today's computerized mumbo jumbo. Lacking a refrigerator, we were forced to visit the local market almost daily. All commodities sold in the market had been hauled there on the backs of Indian *cargadores* (carriers). Women normally did most of the selling and the prices were rarely fixed. It was the custom to haggle over the prices of purchases. The haggling was ordinarily good-humored, the seller secretly willing to lower the asking price and the buyer prepared to raise the bid. Both parties actually seemed to enjoy the dickering and it may well have to be repeated every time the same commodity was purchased from the same vendor for as long as the grass would grow and the rivers flow.

Utterly without a head for business, detesting all forms of shopping, and morbidly reluctant to offend people, I was completely unsuited to marketing. Pat, on the other hand, treated it as an art, and quickly mastered it.

Our lack of a TV set in Comalapa meant that we spent a lot of time socializing with one another and with other human beings, an art that is slowly disappearing in modern America. Whether chatting — during and long after — meals, playing cards or other games, or simply being unobtrusively in one another's company and there if needed, Pat and I interacted on a much deeper level than today's TV viewers, ourselves included, normally do. Without the incessant interruptions for commercials, today's TV addicts might never be aware that another human being was in the same room, much less available for conversation. And in the event that something resembling actual conversation does occur, the meaning of life is seldom deeply probed.

As for the nonexistent telephone, I will confess that except for its usefulness in emergencies, I barely missed it. Today I mostly regard a ringing telephone as an annoying invasion of my precious privacy. Pat bought me a cell phone a few years ago, and, Luddite that I am, I've not yet made a call from it. I'm not even sure that I actually could make one, in the unlikely event that I was so disposed.

Yes, I know these are the views of a hopeless relic of antiquity. But I have also learned that there is a price to be paid for surrendering to the rule of modern personal communications technology. I fear that our growing alienation from the world of nature that I love is largely a consequence of our increasingly powerful infatuation with electronic communication. Let me provide an example: One lovely mid-April morning back in the spring semester of 2009, when I was still teaching, I decided that I'd escape my office and take a walk across campus to savor Mother Nature's splendid display. On the walk from my office to the college library, I probably passed 20 students going here and there. All of them seemed utterly oblivious to the splendors of nature displayed all around us. Each one was engrossed in a cell phone conversation or in text messaging or who knows what else using those little hand-held gadgets with which their generation seems obsessed. To an old grouch like the one I have become, their chatter seemed trifling and inane. Of course, I had no right to impose my values and judgments upon them, but I regretted their apparent lack of appreciation of that spring day's glorious spectacle. My own fondness for birds, flowers, trees, mountains and wildlife is largely a product of my boyhood on a dairy farm in Wisconsin. And it was richly reinforced by my experiences in Guatemala.

Although a small country, no larger than the state of Ohio, Guatemala has remarkable geographic diversity and a rich variety of wildlife. Among its notable geographic features is the vast tropical rain forest in the north, known as El Petén. It also boasts mountain ranges, coastal plains, high plateaus, and a chain of over 30 spectacular volcanic peaks, some of them still active. The forests of Petén are home to an array of exotic animals unknown in my home state of Wisconsin. Jaguars, peccaries, tapirs, monkeys and armadillos are among the species that thrive in that domain of the classic Mayan civilization. For bird lovers, like myself, there are the gorgeous quetzals, the national bird of the republic, as well as multicolored parrots, macaws, toucans, herons and hummingbirds, among other winged creatures. Lake Atitlán, surrounded by mountains in the Department of Sololá, has to be one of the most beautiful lakes in North America. My favorite town in Guatemala, quaint little Antigua, at the base of the mighty Volcan de Agua (Water Volcano) is a place which I always leave with regret. Its bougainvillea-draped walls remain in my memory yet today.

Guatemala is a nature lover's delight and no one respects its natural wonders more than the republic's *gente indigenas* (native people). From Comalapa's Cakchiquel-speaking Indians, I learned to view the natural world in a radically different way, a way that makes all the difference.

Those representative Indian people believe the earth is their sacred mother. They see the universe as an integrated sacred entity and they try to accommodate themselves to its harmonious patterns. They view the sun as their father (sometimes they call him their grandfather) and ask him to shine on all his children: trees, animals, water, human beings, etc. In effect, then, they regard the creatures of the natural world as their brothers and sisters and strive to treat them accordingly. Such deep-seated beliefs do not afford them a convenient justification for the exploitation or destruction of nature's living creatures such as we, who consider them to be subordinate to ourselves and at our service. Those traditional Native

American beliefs are often severely tested by the Indians' struggles for survival in the modern world. But I think that the traditional Indian view of the natural world is the most valuable thing I learned from them while serving in Guatemala.

My PC experiences with Indians in Guatemala stripped away all of the stereotypes and misconceptions that I had nursed about Native Americans. I have never known a better or wiser group of human beings than those Indians among whom Pat, Susie and I lived in the village of San Juan Comalapa, in far-off Guatemala.

AFTERWARDS: THOUGHTS AND PROJECTS

By Dave Snyder

Sally and I left our Guatemalan village of San Vicente and returned to the United States in August 1965. We moved to Cambridge, MA, where I earned my MBA from the Harvard Business School. Sally (who had a degree in teaching and later earned her master's in special education) kept food on the table and paid the rent while I was in school.

I have been in business (mainly international) most of my life, working for multi-nationals, such as W.R. Grace, Nestle, Bausch and Lomb, and Gillette. Sally and I have also run our own businesses for about 20 years, collecting and remanufacturing/recycling inkjet and toner-printer cartridges. We have lived in Colombia, Puerto Rico and Panama. I also commuted/lived in a hotel in Mexico City for three years where Sally and I had our own company.

We are pretty much retired, although I still get involved from time to time with our two sons, who have their own companies in remanufacturing of cartridges. We have five grandchildren whom we see often; our sons and their families live only 15 to 20 minutes from us. Sally gets a kick out of being with our grandchildren and spends a lot of time with them.

I continue to work with Adopt-A-Village, both here in the United States and in Guatemala. (I expect to go to Guatemala three times this year.) I want to get the small coffee growers in San Vicente qualified as organic coffee growers so they can get a higher price for their product. My hot-button issue is birth control. It is imperative that more be done in the San Vicente area, where the average Mayan family has six children.

I have started to work with The Wings Foundation, a nonprofit based in Antigua, started and run by a former Peace Corps volunteer (Colombia in the late 1960s). Wings has accomplished a lot with regard to family planning, not only birth control, but women's health, in the areas around Quetzaltenango, Sololá and southwards. I hope to make use of Wings' expertise in the AAV villages.

Sally and I have also recently become involved with the Colombia Project, which was formed by returned Peace Corps volunteers from South Florida. Their main focus is micro-lending, although they are starting to branch out into nutrition and related areas.

I had a good visit with Mike Schwartz and his wife, when I was in Guatemala in July of last year.

Trip to Guatemala: Adopt-A-Village & Visit to San Vicente Pacaya, our Peace Corps Village

I returned two weeks ago from an 18-day trip to Guatemala. It was my second trip there in the past eight months because I have started working with Adopt-A-Village, which works with Mayans in villages in the Guatemalan highlands, from Barillas, in upper Huehuetenango Department, east to the Mexican border. We inaugurated a small high school, which AAV just finished building. It is the only high school within a 30-to-40 mile radius, which indicates how little the Guatemalan government cares about the Mayans. I spent part of my time at the high school installing solar lights for the student dorms (no electricity in the area).

AAV specializes in education. They have built 10 primary schools. In addition, they have been involved in a variety of Peace Corps-type projects: health-clinic support, chicken-raising, road-building, etc. (Learn more on their website: www.adoptavillage.com

Sally and I are sponsoring three Guatemalan children through AAV. (Check out that program on the website too.)

Visit to San Vicente Pacaya

Sally and I went back to visit our Peace Corps site with our two sons in 1974. I went back on my recent trip and spent most of one day there. Most of the people we worked with in the 1960s had passed away. However, our neighbor and good friend, Regino, was still living in the house across the street from our old Peace Corps home. Regino is now 70 years old and as energetic as a teenager. I could barely keep up with him when he showed me his coffee and vegetable-growing lands.

There is currently a Peace Corps volunteer from California working in San Vicente. He spent most of the day with me. As far as I was able to find out, the Peace Corps has been sending volunteers to work in San Vicente ever since Sally and I left 45 years ago.

Changes I noticed in the village since 1974 include a paved road from the main highway to the village, electricity, and a national park established by a Peace Corps volunteer in 1997 to protect the volcano, Pacaya, which is still active.

UPON RETURNING TO THE STATES

Tim Kraft

It is hard to put into words how profoundly the two years in Guatemala and the journey to the southern tip of the continent afterwards affected my life and outlook. "Transformational" and "educational" come to mind but those experiences were more. They shaped the actions and efforts I would take from then until now. Forty-eight years.

Two parallel tracks form the pattern, although that might suggest a long-range plan, which was not the case.

One track would be political campaigns. President Obama has made the term "community organizer" defined and respectable — at least to most of us. What we did in Guatemala was unique training to complement, in me, an already semi-formed but active interest in politics.

The second track was the newly discovered but ardent interest in all things Latin American. I did not have the slightest idea about how to further this interest but it was there, and it factored into many decisions I would make on the fly.

Upon returning to the United States, I went to the Peace Corps office in Washington and applied for a position in the public affairs division. Hired as a recruiter, I found it easy to organize trips and convey with sincerity (and it never got old) the opportunities that the Peace Corps provided.

Not all students were convinced that this program was putting our country's best foot forward. A growing number, I noticed, were skeptical of what they considered a "Band-Aid public relations ploy," inconsequential, they felt, compared to the escalating war in Vietnam.

While I was lunching at the student union cafeteria at Antioch College in Ohio, the room was galvanized by the student-body president who leapt onto a table, kicked all the trays and dishes off and declared that he was not going to accept his diploma in a week because the university president would not sign an anti-war petition. That was 1966, and things obviously got a little more serious later.

That spring, I applied for and received a Peace Corps scholarship offered by Georgetown University. Latin American studies, of course, was the master's program.

In 1968 I read an ambiguous job notice (in the National Press Club bulletin) about public relations work in Mexico from June to November. That had to be the Olympics. I called my Peace Corps friend Bryce Hamilton and we both got on board, working for the Mexican Olympics Organizing Committee. The committee did a great job preparing and staging the games. But the games were marred by the Mexican government's staging of one of the most secret and violent repressions of student dissidence in its history: the massacre at the Plaza de Tres Culturas.

Most U.S. reporters covered the Olympics with faint praise while they made dire predictions about the altitude, the food, and the readiness of the venues. They missed the government's atrocity almost entirely. Ever since, I have been skeptical of U.S. media coverage of almost anything political in Latin America. But that's a fairly easy attitude to assume, since they cover *hardly anything*.

Political campaigns were becoming my slender fare in California, Indiana, and New Mexico where I had chosen to live. In 1974, I met Governor Jimmy Carter when he campaigned for our candidate in New Mexico; in 1975, I joined Carter's campaign for president.

He appeared to me to be honest, smart, consistent, and indefatigable. He said (in 1974) that he wasn't going to use 1975 to "test the waters," to form an exploratory committee, or see who else was running. He was going to enter every primary and caucus and (direct quote): "I don't intend to lose."

This is the kind of attitude that any campaign coordinator loves to hear, or should want to hear.

Carter had unconventional talking-points, such as human rights, national energy planning, and of all things, a treaty to resolve the growing violence and regional scar that manifested in our relations with Panama. He truly believed (and believes) in the "merits of the case" approach.

I had the good fortune to become his appointments secretary, a position that we reorganized to include all functions of scheduling and advance, daily and weekly schedules, and domestic and international travel. One of our early trips included state visits to Venezuela and Brazil.

Beginning in 1990, my parallel tracks of politics and Latin American interests converged again in an interesting way. That year I participated in an official election observation in El Rama, Nicaragua. The team effort was led by the Guatemalan activist/scholar Jan Knippers Black. It was an exciting and volatile situation. The result was the electoral overthrow of the Sandinistas by the UNO, a coalition led by Violeta Chamorra. Well, let's be candid: The observers thought it was a fair count, but Chamorra was the U.S.-backed candidate and the extraordinary posturing by our government ("Do you want the war to stop?") was not even subtle.

I was an observer in the next two elections in Nicaragua, 1996 and 2002. In the latter two efforts, I ran into my good friend Mike Schwartz (Guatemala III), who was working as a consultant to A.I.D., which reminds me of seeing Jay Jackson in Honduras and Bernie Engel in Colombia. We're everywhere!

There were several other observation trips (first and second rounds, in Peru and Honduras), working with three different organizations: the Carter Center, the OAS, and NDI (National Democratic Institute, a nongovernmental organization based in Washington, DC).

Upon being accepted as an observer, I would try to contact the person most related to the site assignment and say something to the effect, "I speak Spanish and I can handle a jeep. If possible, I'd like to request the most remote possible site, one others may not prefer." That was my blatant attempt to get out of the capital city. I also said I could take a non-Spanish speaker (of which there were several) and that helped my case. I *did* get some remote two-days-to-get-there assignments and felt lucky to do so.

I was rewarded. I saw processes and behavior in remote or rural areas that were truly remarkable because things actually went like they were supposed to go, according to the simple yet explicit instructions that went to the people "out there" in the mountain *aldeas* or the isolated river towns.

This seemed to be worthy of reporting — along with the complexities that occur when rural tabulations are sent to a regional computing center and that, in turn, are transmitted to the national election body, whatever it is called.

I reported on the vote at the grassroots level — the turnout, the basic fairness, and the rigor with which the local officials (often schoolteachers) adhered to the process. First, of course, I'd report to the monitoring organization for which I worked. They, almost without exception, wanted the presidential vote from that site, as soon as it was tabulated.

Then I wrote for the <u>Albuquerque Journal</u>, New Mexico's only statewide daily. The editor wasn't actually enthusiastic about a pre-election situational report, but he OK'd it with a commitment on my part to provide a post-election analysis within 48 hours of the vote. From a remote area, in one Nicaraguan election, I typed it on a manual bulk of a machine and faxed it from the local post office.

It is sad to finish on a down note — there are so many good volunteers in service and I have enjoyed the friendship of the returned Peace Corps volunteers for many years. But let's face the facts: the student-body president at Antioch College is still very relevant.

As an organization of RPCVs lobbies and struggles (an Internet campaign) to increase the Peace Corps budget by a few *million* dollars, and would count it a victory to hold at $440 million...well, you do the math. What percent of $550 *billion* (the Department of Defense's annual budget, that Congress guesses at) is the figure the Peace Corps requests to barely keep the doors open?

We all understand the legitimate need for a strong defense in a chaotic and violent world. But when you compare the efforts for peaceful outreach versus the carte blanche acceptance of preemptive warfare, I think our nation's priorities are badly warped.

APPENDIX I

No member of Guatemala III better personifies the adventurous spirit and compassion of our group than the fun-loving and tender-hearted Betsy Markland Schwartz. The following account is based on excerpts from her letters back home while bicycling through the Middle East with other women cyclists on their "Pedal For Peace" tour in the Fall of 2009.

Betsy

FOLLOW THE WOMEN/PEDAL FOR PEACE

By Betsy Markland Schwartz

October 1, 2009

"Sabaah Alkhair! Izzayak?"
"Ana kwayisa, alhamdulilah!!"

For those of you who have not yet learned Arabic, the above expressions are a typical greeting and response. They mean, "Good Morning. How are you?" "I am fine, thanks be to God." Yes, I have been studying Arabic as much as I can in my spare time. And I now have a vocabulary of about 60 words at my command! Like a two year old! Tomorrow I will attempt to learn how to read and write the Arabic alphabet so I can sound out words on signs — hopefully!

But the purpose of this letter is to be informative and to help you understand what has been going on during these last 4 weeks. First, I am thrilled to report that I far surpassed my goal of raising $3,000 towards the building of a playground for the children of Gaza. With help from each of you, I collected $4,271.00!!! YES, more than $1,000 over my goal. And all of the five others on our California team surpassed their goals. Collectively, we raised over $14,000!!! We are so proud of all of our donors!! You have inspired us to learn as much as we can through reading, viewing documentaries, and having professionally-led group workshops so we will be able to contribute, and absorb as much as possible on this incredible journey.

Our California section of the American team has been busy! In early September, we were introduced to Dr. Moyara Ruehsen, Associate Professor at the Monterey Institute of International Studies. Dr. Ruehsen graciously agreed to come to my house and give us a special presentation on "Cross-Cultural Communication in the Middle East," introducing us to some basic cultural customs such as eating with your right hand only (I am left-handed!). Hugging is to be avoided and an older woman must give a limp handshake to a man or she may be taken as being too forward or aggressive! Of course, polite Arabic greetings as well as appropriate attire were also discussed. We had a fun time learning! A highlight of the evening was the Middle-Eastern dinner, including hummus, an eggplant-dish, chicken-kabobs, chickpeas, yogurt and pita bread along with mint tea! It was a great educational experience for us all.

The second week in September we hired Nabil, a Tunisian, who teaches Arabic at the Center for non-violence here in Santa Cruz. The course that he teaches will not start until after we leave, so our group of six hired him for one session on basic emergency expressions. You know, older women (and older men too) always need to know how to ask, "Where's the bathroom?" Actually, we are curious about where the bathroom is going to be for 300 women on bikes. I remember when I cycled through Vietnam, we just had to stop right on the side of the highway and try and hide behind the berm of a rice paddy!! We won't be so lucky as to have rice paddies in the Middle East! Remember to ask me about that when it's over! Anyway, Nabil kindly agreed to meet us at Janet's house where we had an hour-long lesson in Arabic greetings. Afterwards, we practiced what we had learned over another tasty Middle-Eastern dinner.

The third week in September had us practicing some "Mind-clearing techniques" presented to us in a workshop by Dr. Donna Montgomery, who has been trained specifically in dealing with groups who are exposed to many stresses. She taught us how to rely on dyads whereby we will be able to help each other deal with any issues we may have, either before we leave next week or after we are on the trip. It is a marvelous way to share and unload the brain without putting any burden on the partner. The partner simply has to listen, without saying a thing, and understand. Donna is a new cyclist in our club and was able to show appreciation to us for our support of her bike-riding by offering us this professional workshop. We processed our learning over a Betsy-made delicious chicken salad and olive-bread lunch followed by the most scrumptious almond and dark-chocolate cookies from Trader Joe's.

Just yesterday we had our fourth and last gathering as a team. It started with a visit by a Santa Cruz Sentinel reporter and photographer. We had a fun interview and then began our meeting, which was to discuss everyone's emotional stress level and the issue of what to take on the trip. Our emotions have been very much like a roller coaster! I am quite positive and have been pretty much on a HIGH the entire time. Some of the others have had fears about certain things. Although I cannot make their fears go away, I can reassure them that my trip last year to the Middle East to build houses with Habitat in Jordan and my ensuing trip into Syria and Jerusalem were filled with nothing but kindness from everyone I met. From my limited exposure, I have found Middle Easterners to be very warm and open. They commonly invite me to experience their culture. We topped off our discussion with a California-Kitchen pair of pizzas and a green dinner salad. (You knew there was going to be a meal mentioned, right?)

254

We leave on Monday morning, October 5th, to head to Beirut, Lebanon, a flight of some twenty-four hours. Fortunately, we have given ourselves a little time before the Pedal for Peace event begins on Oct 8th. From the bottom of my heart, I thank each and everyone of you for your interest and support. So many of you sent lovely encouraging notes with your donation. Thank you. I will send brief reports to you on the trip, if possible, but most likely I will send a follow-up letter with some photos after I return home on Nov 4th. (I will be going to Turkey to visit friends for two weeks after the completion of Pedal for Peace.)

And now I must finish the most difficult part of the whole trip — PACKING!!! And the great thing about it is that undoubtedly most of those 300 other women scattered all over the world are experiencing substantially the same issues that I am. Now doesn't that make the world seem quite small and united?

Peace to all. Ma' asalaama.

Betsy

Note: Several people have asked if we will do a blogspot. Well, fortunately, a friend will work with us and manage a blogspot for us. It is up and running. And you can send comments. As time and internet opportunities permit, we may all send some emails to be posted on this blog. The Blog URL: www.pedal-4peacesc.wordpress.com

October 7, 2009

It's a long way to Beirut! About 35 hours!! The Monday 6 AM flight from San Francisco to JFK was memorable for me because the young woman sitting next to me coughed — on me — the ENTIRE FLIGHT!!

JoAnn, sitting 2 rows behind me, had a healthier seatmate!

We met Jane at JFK, as scheduled, and continued our 10-hour flight to Istanbul. A few movies, lots of chat time, and a couple of hours of sleep later we arrived at Istanbul feeling energized.

With a 12 hour-layover, we caught a shuttle into Istanbul and added 3 more people to an already crowded city of 20 million. Jane and I introduced JoAnn to a few of the city's highlights: the Blue Mosque, the Aya Sofia Museum, and the Cisterns– all three ancient historical-sites. A rooftop restaurant provided sights of beautiful cascading domed-roofs and minarets as we dined on lamb and beef-kabobs and salads. Autumn colors under a cloudless blue sky completed the picture.

Returning to Istanbul's Ataturk Airport, we sleepily waited 4 more hours for our Turkish Air flight 1226 to Beirut, Lebanon. Promptly at 9:45 PM, Tuesday, Oct 6, we departed on the last leg of our excursion to take us to the starting line of Pedal for Peace. Thirty minutes before landing it was announced that we should take our seats for the remainder of the flight as we were flying over a big storm. I opened the window shade to find a spectacular 3/4 moon and a star studded-sky above a layer of thick white clouds. They were just a bit off to the left of the plane. And then I saw the lightning! It was indeed spectacular! It seemed that every 2 or 3 seconds there would be a new strike. It was like watching a movie — all off to the left. We began our descent — all the while the clouds and lightning performed to the left and the moon and stars watched from above. As we approached Beirut I could see the Mediterranean below us, lightning to our left, and a line of yellow lights along the sea coast. The lights climbed up into the hills, the beautiful mountains of Beirut. The whole city of half a million people right on the edge of the Mediterranean, was alight as we approached. We made a smooth landing with one of our wings almost touching the sea.

Our greatest joy was finding Samar standing outside the arrivals-gate holding a paper with the names of Jane DeJarnette, Betsy Schwartz and JoAnn Smith written on it. We had arrived! Our 36 hours of travel was at a beautiful end. We were transported to the Legend Hotel for a well-deserved night of sleep.

It's a long way to Beirut, but we're here. And we are numbers 8, 9 and 10 of the approximately 200 anticipated women who will be arriving in the next 24 hours.

October 8, 2009

This morning Jane, JoAnn and I went down to our hotel's complimentary breakfast after a good sleep. After we had finished eating and were sitting at the table talking, a woman about 45 or so came to our table and asked, "Are you Pedal for Peace?" "Yes," we answered. She began explaining that she was a Ph.D. from Iraq and was in Beirut for 10 days with a group of her students teaching them about business. She likes to take her students to other countries where they can feel a little bit of freedom. She then asked if we "could go to Iraq to pedal for the peace of Iraq?"

How wonderful it would be if the power of the pedal could bring such peace!

The woman then asked if one of her male-students could be photographed with us to enjoy the freedom of being with uncovered women. We agreed.

This evening we will celebrate Jane's 73rd birthday by taking her to a lovely beach restaurant where we will all sample the waterpipe — we were told last night by a group of young university women that the grape-flavored *nargila* (waterpipe) is the best!

Oh, yes, the teams are now beginning to form. We just met the Italian team and the Austrian team. I don't think we will have so much time for writing after tomorrow.

Enjoy yourselves, as we certainly are, over here in this wonderfully vibrant city of Beirut.

October 13, 2009

This is coming to you from the business center in the five-star Ebla Cham Palace Hotel in Damascus, Syria.

Everything has been incredible. There is so much to say, but I have only ten minutes on this computer. So please excuse the mistakes.

As for the question of where to go to the bathroom — the answer: Wherever you can! As long as it is not outside! Or if it is outside, you must make sure that no one spots you!! Women do not go to the bathroom outdoors! So we must hope that someone will offer their house to us, which is what usually happens. It seems the one thing forgotten here is that 200 women riding bikes all day long need to GO!!

I had a wonderful encounter with a Syrian family yesterday while cycling. I was climbing up a big hill along with everyone else when I spotted two sheep along the side of the road. Since the sheep were different from the usual scenery, I stopped to photograph them and an entire family appeared. They were happy to pose for the camera and then they gave me a pomegranate. It hit the spot with its moist juicy fruit, as it was so very hot! In return, I gave the family a small gift of a keychain with the word California on it. They were so grateful that they gave me another pomegranate. It was a lovely exchange and it all happened despite my limited vocabulary of Arabic!

Each day a small positive incident happens. It is wonderful.

There are some sad things happening also, as each day brings several accidents. The topography is very hilly, which means some long descents. We have many women who have very limited experience on a bike. They are not familiar with changing gears or using the brakes. Sadly, many have used just the left or front brake and there have been a handful of "over the handlebars" accidents.

The security is incredible. The places we are staying at night and the meals we have been served are really gorgeous and full-flavored!!

My time on the computer is up. I must go. There is a line of women waiting for it. I am making new friends from all over the world. The teams here are awesome and I love what is happening in the towns as we come cycling through. The entire town awaits us with water and snacks. The children are all there in their pink and blue school uniforms.

I will write when I can but not for a while, I imagine.

October 15, 2009

We arrived in Amman, the capital of Jordan, last night about midnight after an incredible entrance into the country. I will describe it briefly. There is so much more I could say, but I have such a short time to write. We are up at 7 every morning but don't make it to bed until about 2:00 AM. We are on the bike or the bus or at a ceremony or involved in some activity every minute, so I have little time to even think!! But I will do the best I can in the twinkling of an eye. Please forgive any mistakes. I thank all of you who have written to me. I love hearing from you.

We got to the Jordanian border about 8 PM, leaving Syria behind, and were greeted by four military men riding camels and by a large marching band. We got off the bus and followed a grand procession of blaring music, dancing and hooting all about. Photographs were being taken all around us, and the cameramen were taking pictures of whatever we did. The procession led us across the Jordanian border! Never in all my 130 countries have I had such a border crossing!!

The city of Amman, built on seven hills, has a population of about 3 million. This morning we left on our bikes, with a police escort. We cycled about 30 kilometers (18 miles) up and down the hills of Amman, with all the traffic alongside of us. Please remember, a large number of the cyclists here have very little experience on a bicycle and when it comes to a hill, they stop right at its base and start walking. It is the American team's responsibility to ask them to please move to the right so the others can pass them! And with all the traffic, it was an amazing sight for the city this morning. We safely arrived at the University of Jordan, which had kindly prepared a cultural function of traditional dances as well as some speeches by the President and the Director of International studies who made a short speech about PEACE. "If men have the ability to make a war and a truce, then the women have the ability to make the peace," is how he began. He thanked all of us for our efforts on behalf of peace. A lovely lunch followed the ceremony.

Our next event was to get back on the bikes and fight the city's traffic toward the citadel. Many annoyed faces glared at us as we poked along on their major thoroughfares. We caused them great delays in their daily stressful commutes across the overcrowded city. A lovely Roman ruin and theater as well a kite-flying demonstration for peace awaited us. An NGO working with children living in the community around the Roman ruin had directed a large group of Palestinian children to make fifty kites. They made them with the designs of the flags of all the countries included. But it took a great deal of convincing for these twelve and thirteen- year-old boys to make a flag for the USA. After much teasing, Ahmad had decided to take on the unpopular task of making the American-flag kite. Each kite was about 4 feet square with a tail about 20 feet long. They were gorgeous. Our job was to work in groups of two and decorate the kites with peace symbols and expressions. Then the boys would help us tie the strings on them and teach us to fly them. Jane worked with 12-year-old Ahmad on his kite. He asked her to write for him a message to President Obama. His statement read: "Hello Mr. Obama. We are humans too, and we want peace. Ahmad. We deserve PEACE. "

And so on and on it goes. Every day we learn more stories and talk to more people. I have many wonderful photos, but unfortunately I can't send them from this hotel. When I get home, I will be able to send some of the most meaningful, and I will include Ahmad and his kite!!

Tomorrow we leave Amman and cycle to the Dead Sea. Apparently, there is quite a descent to get there and only experienced riders are permitted to cycle that section. On Saturday we head into West Bank, Palestine, for the last four days. I don't think there will be much time to be on the internet. Stay well everyone. This is truly an incredible journey I am on. There is so much to say and so little time to write.

16 October, 8:30AM.

We were given 30 extra minutes before leaving for the King Hussein Gardens for some peace games. After that we will begin the cycling to the Dead Sea.

So, I have just a few minutes before we take off and I wanted to sketch what our group looks like to the normal passer-by:

We are a huge group! Two hundred women require a lot of care: First in our long line of vehicles, is the ambulance, with the siren screaming, of course! Next are about four or five police SUV's. And, of course, we have the MEDIA! About five or six cars full. Next in our procession are six Greyhound-style busses. Predictably, we have a cadre of motorcycle police, all motoring up and down past the long line of vehicles, making sure all is well.

And we find ourselves in such processions every time we have to board the buses!! Sometimes we are a part of them very briefly as we are escorted to a START POINT for cycling. At other times, such as during the border crossings or when covering such long distances as between northern Syria and Damascus, the procession may last four or more hours. The Americans, Austrians, Finns, Estonians, and Greeks are on one bus. (Oh, there is a team from Iran here, but I have not found them to take their photograph.)

Now you have a picture of what we look like when we move!! Imagine when a few women start saying they need to go to the bathroom, and the poor bus driver must communicate by radio with all vehicles, and they must find a place big enough along the side of the highway for ALL vehicles to PARK, and let the women out!! So, there you have it!!   And now we're off to the Gardens!

Thursday, Oct 23, 2009

Crossing the Border to Jericho in the West Bank, Palestine

Last Saturday started with an early morning float in the warm salty Dead Sea, followed by a typical Middle-Eastern breakfast of pita bread, hummus, olives, tomatoes, cucumbers, cheeses, yogurt, mashed-beans with olive oil, and hard-boiled eggs. On this particular morning we had a tearful farewell as teams of women from Lebanon, Syria, Iran, and some of the Jordanians and Palestinians remained while we departed for the King Hussein/Allenby Bridge border crossing. Due to the political tensions between the Arab states and the Israelis, there can be no crossing into Israel for citizens of the Arab nations, except for some Jordanians with a special passport. Some of the Palestinian team presently live in other Arab nations and therefore had no permission to pass.

We arrived at Jordan's border well before the 11 AM deadline for passing out of Jordan and into Israel. On Fridays and Saturdays the borders close at 1 PM. All went smoothly leaving Jordan. Our bikes were trucked across the border by our Lebanese bike-service men. They were given special permission to drive the bikes across the Israeli border and drop them there as a Lebanese truck cannot enter

Israel. The plan called for the 130 women to cycle to Jericho after crossing into Israel.

We entered Passport Control and all of us disembarked and entered the building to get our visas for Israel . Many people were already in lines. We joined, after a potty break, of course, and slowly, slowly inched along in line. We thought it strange when every once in a while one or two women would be rejected and asked to sit in a chair against the wall, without the passport! By the end of our line, sitting against the wall were: four Australians (the whole team!), one Japanese (out of a team of twelve), two of the four-member Turkish team, one French woman, one Austrian, three Danes (of the 18-member team), and Detta — the founder of Follow the Women, who stayed behind with the unfortunate twelve! The more than 110 of us who had passed through now filled the small hall on the other side of Passport Control. And there we waited! Two more hours passed! It was 3 PM. NOTHING had happened with our twelve. They were all there sitting and wondering "WHY?" A bit later we got word that the two Turkish women were refused entry because they had neglected to get their necessary visa. In addition, Detta could do nothing to help them as just three days before, the government of Turkey had insulted Israel and relations were already strained. The French woman was a French-Moroccan traveling with the French team but on a Moroccan passport (an Arab nation = no entry!). Nothing could be done. Those three unfortunates left on a bus back to Jordan. And now Detta was being labeled a political activist, the leader of a cult called "Follow the Women," and her passport was taken also! A total of ten women were left behind, unable to cross with us!

What did the big group do? SING!! We began singing in an effort to give hope to our ten rejected friends who really had no idea why they were being detained. No information was given to them. Two more hours passed. We were still singing. Israeli security was now enjoying our singing and dancing and they smiled and took photos of us. The 10 detainees were still wondering. "Is it because we have brand new passports?" wondered the Australians. "Is it because I travel too much?" wondered Mio, a young Japanese adventure-cyclist who had once disguised herself as a boy and cycled solo from Kenya to South Africa. "Is it because we have done too much traveling in Eastern Europe?" wondered the Danes. No one understood what was happening. And then suddenly at 5:30 p.m., when it was nearly dark, ten passports were handed over to the detainees. Everyone broke into song and danced. The cameras began to roll and each woman danced out through the turnstile into freedom! Fun videos were taken by all of the happiness of being released. But no explanation of any type was ever given for the detentions.

"Ladies, on the bikes!" yelled Mark over the megaphone. It was nearly 6 PM when we got rolling, almost completely dark. We had 8 kilometers (5 miles) to cycle — all uphill to Jericho. The bus driver did his best to give us a little light as the 130 women began to climb up the hill. We passed through the three checkpoints with no problem. The Israelis had called ahead to clear us. Under a pitch-black sky we entered Jericho to loud cheers from hundreds of people who had been waiting hours for our arrival. They lavished us with drinking-water and dates and a Palestinian flag. We then cycled on a short distance in the dark to a wonderful dinner of upside-down chicken, a warm welcome-speech by the mayor of Jericho, and to our delight, a bus ride to the hotel.

Jane and I left at 4 AM for two weeks in Turkey. I promise to write at least two more entries as soon as I can. This is such an incredible and informative journey.

I returned home Nov 5th early in the morning and slept the next 13 hours. I got up, ate a little food, visited with one of my friends who had also been on Pedal for Peace, went back to bed, and now it is 2 AM on Nov 6th and I can sleep no longer. So I will take pen to paper and write to you all!

There is so much to say! I will begin with a little history of Follow the Women, Pedal for Peace. The founder, Detta Reagan, 58, was formerly a firefighter and then an air traffic controller at Manchester, England's busy airport. She left those careers and for years now has been working with disadvantaged youth groups from conflicted areas around the world. The Middle East was her area of specialization. It involved her with Syrian, Lebanese, Jordanian and Palestinian youth groups. She found she had a strong desire to "do something" to improve the lives of the people she met there. Being an avid cyclist, she felt that getting many women to cycle in the Middle East, where women typically do not do so, would surely bring attention to the problems confronted by women and children. Thus, in 2002, Follow the Women, Pedal for Peace was launched. Detta, believing change will come from women, has offered this ride five times since 2004 to teams of women from any country in the world. April of 2011 is the scheduled departure date for its next excursion.

This year approximately two-hundred women from almost thirty different countries participated.

Each team was allowed to have up to twenty members. The Syrian team pushed the envelope with twenty-two, while Denmark followed closely behind with eighteen women. By contrast, Finland's team was made up of a single woman! The USA team, with the oldest average age, had eleven members, six coming from our Santa Cruz County Cycling Club and five from NY or MA. The cutest team (in my opinion) was made up of twelve delightful young Japanese women who wowed the entire group when they all appeared in their beautiful kimonos at our first night's opening ceremony in Beirut.

We were women ranging in age from sixteen to seventy-four. We were mothers and daughters, sisters, friends, political activists, teachers, lawyers, students, retired women, all with different levels of cycling ability. Many had little previous experience on a bike. We were of various colors and sizes; some were completely covered and others wore cycling shorts and short-sleeved shirts; but we all wore helmets! We also shared a common purpose: an interest in doing whatever small bit we could to help promote peace in the Middle East. One woman cannot do much to achieve our goal, but perhaps a large group of women can. We were all told that our mission was to Go, to See, to Tell, and, finally, to Act. With this letter, I am beginning TO TELL.

We pedaled some 450 kilometers (270 miles) through the Middle Eastern countries of Lebanon, Syria, Jordan and Palestine. We pedaled up hills so steep that women were constantly jumping off their bikes and walking! We pedaled down mountains so sheer that women were flying over their handle bars and landing on their heads, not realizing the power of the front brake! We pedaled into towns and villages where hundreds of people, who had been waiting for hours, lined the sides of the roads, handing us flowers, snacks and/or bottles of water. We pedaled under welcome banners to daily lunches where the mayors would address us, where community developers would greet us, and where neighborhood representatives shared their stories with us. We went to nightly receptions at universities, in large hotels, in political headquarters; and we listened to political leaders welcome us and thank us for coming to see how their people live.

Our last four days in Palestine's West Bank took us to Jericho, Hebron, East Jerusalem, Al Ram, Ramallah, and last of all to Bil'een. We endured the hottest temperature yet, 100° F daily, and we found it difficult to get enough drinking water to keep us hydrated. As it was impossible to do the entire trip on bikes, we were able to ride buses through certain areas of the West Bank. We passed many sections of the 26-foot-high, almost 400-mile long separation wall. From the bus we were able to see many of the Israeli settlements built atop the surrounding hills.

One afternoon we cycled to the Hebron District and experienced a long wait at a checkpoint as we tried to enter the Old City of Hebron. We had been told that we would cycle to Hebron if we could get in. (We did.) Thereafter, we were to cycle in the Old City of Hebron if we were allowed in. (We weren't.) But while we were singing and waiting at the checkpoint, Reem, the principal of a school of 160 children, ages six to sixteen, tried to help us past the checkpoint. She related that she and her students must go through this checkpoint (metal detector and turnstile) twice daily to get to school on the other side. She explained to us that since there are 500 Israeli settlers living on the other side of the checkpoint on Ash-Shuhada Street, the main thoroughfare, Arabs are not allowed to walk there. She and her students were forced to detour and take the long way around, through the cemetery. I observed several doors in the area with a red or blue Star of David. Reem explained that the resident Arab families had been removed from these homes as they were located too close to the checkpoint. The homes now remain completely abandoned in a state of disrepair. Four armed Israeli soldiers stood on the rooftop looking down upon our group. Rejected, we returned to the bikes and cycled away.

Some Facts: Hebron District, the largest in the West Bank, is 50% smaller now than in 1948. Outside the city there are twenty-five Israeli settlements, with ten new smaller settlements called "Outposts" being built atop the surrounding hills. New roads have been built to connect these settlements with the city and beyond. However, these roads are only for Israelis to use; Palestinians must use the old roads. Inside the city there are fourteen checkpoints and fifty roadblocks. 40,000 Palestinians live inside the Old City of Hebron. 500 Israeli settlers with 5,000 soldiers or guards protecting them, also live in the city, on the holy street, Ash-Shuhada, where Palestinians are no longer allowed to walk.

At a later date we cycled seventeen kilometers, uphill and down, from Ramallah to Bil'een, a city divided by the separation wall. For more than four years, the people there have tried to halt the growth of the settlements and remove the electrified fence that divides their city by leaving their olive orchards on the other side of the fence. After the midday Friday prayer ritual, a large group of the townspeople walk with the Imam to the fenced off area where they stand in protest and pray. I learned that much earlier the residents of Bil'een had chained themselves to their olive trees for 3 months to keep the Israelis from cutting down their trees. That halted the cutting for a while. Then as the settlement-building continued (the plan is to bring 150,000 settlers to this area), the townspeople constructed a trailer home in the middle of the settlement to enable their people to stay there also. The Israelis said that a trailer was only a temporary building and they would be back the next day to destroy it. The townspeople got together and within fourteen hours were able to build a permanent structure. When the Israelis returned to take down the trailer, they found a permanent structure which they were not allowed to destroy. This caused a further halt in the construction projects. The conflict still continues as the townspeople do everything possible to halt the cutting of their olive orchards, and to halt the construction of the separation wall and settlements.

After lunch, served by the generous people of this town, we rode our bikes to the area of protest. We found many exploded tear-gas canisters (actually, I picked up one that was unexploded. I immediately, and very carefully, placed it back on the ground) and observed the Israeli soldiers across the electrified fence as they watched our every move. A nervous farmer whose land is surrounded by this fence on 3 sides came and locked his gate so we could not trespass on his property. He was afraid the Israelis would think we were his friends and there might be retaliation after we left. A large group of us stood at the fence and sang, while the children who had followed us yelled, "WE WANT PEACE!" in the direction of the soldiers. I wish that we had had the opportunity to go into Israel and listen to people there tell their side of the story. Perhaps that will be next.

This trip has had a profound impact on me. I began to understand, through what I saw and heard, how difficult it is to live under occupation. With the road closures, the checkpoints, the soldiers, the separation wall, the settlements, the cutting of the olive trees, the lack of freedom to move, the lack of basic services, it is all so difficult. Much too difficult!

I would like to end with a positive short story about how one man and one woman found peace through love:

Nancy, an Israeli horse-trainer, went to an international horse competition where she met Hassan, a Palestinian. Hassan found her very attractive, both in looks and in her expertise with horses; so he invited her to come to Jericho where he had a horse farm. "Shaking and so nervous she was almost yellow," Hassan explained with laughing eyes, "she came to my farm." Nancy soon agreed to visit on a monthly basis to train Hassan's horses. Soon Hassan asked her to do the training on a weekly basis. And then, soon after, he asked her to marry him! They have now been happily married 10 years. The first five were kept a secret from everyone. Recently, at a USAID ceremony, she shared her story publicly for the first time, by announcing, "This is my Palestinian husband, Hassan." Theirs' is a wonderful love story about one way to make peace!

I am extremely grateful to you, my donors, for your support and interest. You made me feel so proud of our "CA girls'" (as we were lovingly referred to) collective contribution of almost $14,000, the largest any country has raised. It was used for the construction of one or more playgrounds in Gaza, with money also allotted for maintenance. We were able to see two other much-used Follow the Women playgrounds (Jericho and Ramallah) built with Follow the Women (FTW) money. They appeared to be well-constructed and cared for. We met some of the people in charge of the building, and they assured us the project in Gaza will begin very soon. I am both delighted and honored that we will have done that project together. Thank you so much for your very generous donations.

APPENDIX II

Charles "Chuck" Davenport was a quiet, unassuming Texan, who completed Peace Corps training with our Guatemala III group but never made it to Guatemala. An illness prevented him from departing with the rest of us from the United States in January, 1964. Soon thereafter a serious automobile accident, which severely damaged his spinal cord, left him in a wheelchair and unable to serve in Guatemala. He was a very likeable young man who is remembered fondly by Tim Kraft in the following personal recollection:

A REMEMBRANCE OF CHUCK DAVENPORT
By Tim Kraft

Chuck Davenport and Bernie Engel had an adjoining room to Doug Tabor and myself in training.

In the December interim after training and before departure, Chuck was diagnosed with hepatitis (or amebic dysentery? My bad memory...) and was unable to leave for Guatemala.

In 1964, Chuck was in a bad car accident (as a passenger, asleep, in the back seat) that damaged his spinal cord and consigned him to hospitals and a wheel chair. I saw him twice in the 70's, once in a care center and once at his home in Jacksonville, Cherokee County, East Texas. He had an identifying characteristic or anecdote about each setting.

We had a running football bet—Washington Redskins vs. Dallas Cowboys — for many years. It was straight up, no line, and I probably lost most of them, except for the Joe Gibbs era. Big bucks: five dollars every time. He had once started a small business: a nutrition and health food store, but it didn't last very long.

In the early 90's, I came home one night and listened to our primitive answering machine say something like this: "this is Chuck Davenport's brother, and he passed away a few days ago. I thought you would want to know." No name, no number, no details. I knew he had lost his father, and his mother's name yielded a "disconnect" message.

That is, in effect, "what happened." What follows is a sort of personal recollection. You will recall, I'm sure, a wiry, sandy-haired guy, about 5'11", really low-key, with an easy smile. Hell, I remember the voice as clear as a bell...and the poker games in the dorm. He was a cool player, but not a lucky one, as I'm sure Bernie Engel will recall.

He and I discovered early on a mutual desire to get assigned to El Petén in Guatemala. And through contrived remarks and amateur lobbying, we made Keni and Tony, our CARE supervisors, aware of it.

274

Toward the end of training, we had a positive anticipation that we would get it.

Two things happened in training that were, in retrospect, bad omens for our hoped-for Peace Corps experience.

One, I dislocated my shoulder in the NMSU pool, and the wing-nut doctor assigned to our group couldn't "reduce" it (get it back in place) on the spot. (An emergency room doctor in Las Cruces did it in five minutes.) But the PC doc subsequently recommended to Paul Duffield that I be dismissed from the program for a "physical disability."

I spent a frantic couple of days (just before the Chihuahua field trip) lining up a doctor, any doctor, who could "fix" the shoulder while the group went to Mexico. My criteria were "cheap" and "available" and I found one who said he could do it in a VA hospital in El Paso. Paul Duffield, God bless him, said that he'd find a way to cover the bill (about 500 or 600 dollars in 1963). It worked.

Second omen: Chuck almost left the program of his own volition. I came back to our rooms after hearing of JFK's assassination to find Chuck packing to leave. He was, like all of us, devastated...but he assumed that it was a Texas right-winger who had done it...and he was wracked by a pain and humiliation that, somehow, in his own mind, being "a Texan" made him unfit to continue with our training. I pleaded with him to stay in the program, and, again, an incomplete memory tells me that Bernie, Dave Siebert, and Mike Schwartz joined in. As events and the news unfolded, we watched the developments (and Chuck) like a hawk. He began to reconsider. But don't think for a moment that it was an idle or theatrical gesture on his part to leave.

That's about it for me. I had all the luck, with the Petén assignment, a good partner in Carol Bellamy, and a great experience. Chuck, for his part, never conveyed an iota of self-pity or a single "what if" in our calls and correspondence. That should come as a surprise to no one.

I'm sure most of you will have your own recollections. He was a deep-down decent person, the kind of partner (or ambassador) that Carolyn Plage recalled from the field trip to Mexico.

Or, to keep it simple, I do remember clearly the first ten minutes meeting him in the NMSU dorms — this is one likeable hombre.

APPENDIX III

THE STUPIDITY OF WAR

By Evelyn Brubaker Glasscock

In October, 2007, I had the opportunity to travel to Bosnia and Herzegovina and Croatia with a group of women on a Woman-to-Woman mission journey of The Christian Church (Disciples of Christ).

We visited various sites with projects aided by Church World Service and The Christian Church's outreach program, Week of Compassion. These projects are to aid the people of Bosnia and Herzegovina in "getting back on their feet" again after the terrible destruction inflicted on the country by the war of "ethnic cleansing" in the mid 90's. The people we were privileged to meet are tirelessly involved in efforts to get the economy going and in helping each other heal. They are courageous and resolved in their determination to help those who are in Bosnia and Herzegovina now and those who are refugees but would love to go back to Bosnia and Herzegovina if there were places to live and jobs available.

What problems are ever solved by picking up guns and shooting at each other? Especially in a civil war, such as in Bosnia and Herzegovina. What possible satisfaction or feelings of success can people have — even those considered the victors — when they have ruined their country's economy, infrastructure, homes, lives, and livelihoods? Those were the questions that continually went through my mind as we traveled around the country and saw destroyed buildings everywhere and learned of projects in which the people were trying to make a little money by participating in chicken and milk projects, and by making rugs and doing beautiful needle work (for which there was no market), etc. My answer was "NONE!"

In 1981 I returned to Guatemala for the first time after my Peace Corps years there, and I remember asking the same questions. Why in the world were Guatemalans killing other Guatemalans? Why were they destroying lives and property there in that beautiful country? It made me sick to see soldiers everywhere, fear on faces, and uneasiness among the people I had grown to care about deeply when I lived there as a PCV. I was even caught in a guerrilla attack in Chichicastenango myself; but I was able to escape — unlike the people I saw in the market with fear and anxiety on their faces, who had no place to run to.

Back in western Bosnia and Herzegovina in the municipality of Grahovo I saw the beneficial efforts of those working with the "Build a Village" programs.

They were working on restoring a means to make a living through milk production, among other things. After meeting with some of the leaders of the town, 97% of whose infrastructure was destroyed in the war, we visited with the nurse in the medical center. She was very frustrated because she didn't have the equipment necessary to do her job. She could draw blood, for example, but she had no lab for testing it.

One day we visited homes in groups of two or three of those of us involved in the projects of "Build a Village." In the first home I met a woman who has a vision for Bosnia. She wants to build a B&B (two bungalows) on the hill beside her house overlooking the beautiful countryside because she's looking toward a future when lots of tourists visit her country once again. She wants to be ready for them when they come. In contrast, in the second home I visited I saw despair in a man who wants desperately to work and earn a living for his family again, but he cannot find a job. There are very few jobs to be had.

I saw the same hopes, struggles, and sometimes sadness, as I visited with the members of two women's clubs. The women are helping each other to heal and are there for each other to share the burdens. They provide child care for those who have jobs, and they work on projects together to help themselves economically.

Before I went to Bosnia and Herzegovina, and again since returning home, I read Zlata's Diary written by Zlata Filipovic. Zlata was eleven when she started keeping her diary, and she was living in Sarajevo when it was under siege. In her entry for Monday, April 20, 1992, she writes:

> War is no joke, it seems. It destroys, kills, burns, separates, brings unhappiness. Terrible

shells fell today on Basiarsiga, the old town center. Terrible explosions. We went down into the cellar, the cold, dark, revolting cellar. And ours isn't even all that safe. Mommy, Daddy, and I just stood there holding on to one another in a corner that looked safe. Standing there in the dark, in the warmth of my parents' arms, I thought about leaving Sarajevo. Everybody is thinking about it…. I have decided we should stay here together. Tomorrow I'll tell Keka that you have to be brave and stay with those you love and those who love you. I can't leave my parents, and I don't like the other idea of leaving my father behind alone either.

The entry for Tuesday, May 5, 1992, states: "… we've arranged things in the apartment. My room and Mommy and Daddy's are too dangerous to be in. They face the hills, which is where they're shooting from."

In the entry for Monday, June 29, 1992, Zlata tells about the horrors of war and their effect on her life:

BOREDOM!!! SHOOTING!!! SHELLING!!! PEOPLE BEING KILLED!!! DESPAIR!!! HUNGER!!! MISERY!!! FEAR!!! That's my life! The life of an innocent eleven-year-old schoolgirl!! A schoolgirl without a school, without the fun and excitement of school. A child without games, without friends, without the sun, without birds, without nature, without fruit, without chocolate or sweets, with just a little powdered milk. In short, a child without a childhood. A wartime child. I now realize that I am really living through a war. I am witnessing an ugly, disgusting war.

I and thousands of other children in this town that is being destroyed, that is crying, weeping, seeking help, but getting none. God, will this ever stop, will I ever be a schoolgirl again, will I ever enjoy my childhood again? I once heard that childhood is the most wonderful time of your life. And it is. I loved it, and now an ugly war is taking it all away from me. Why? I feel sad. I feel like crying. I am crying.[3]

There is much more from Zlata as things worsen in Sarajevo and friends and relatives are killed as the war rages on.

On our journey to Bosnia and Herzegovina our group was invited to attend sessions of the Tanenbaum Peacemakers Conference which was taking place in Sarajevo at that time. One evening we heard the Pontanima Interfaith Choir, made up of people of all races, religions, ethnic groups, etc. They sang together with beautiful harmony. We heard speakers who were Jewish, Orthodox, Islamic, Catholic, Protestant, Evangelical; and all said basically the same things. We had dinner with people from around the world who had come to Sarajevo for the conference.

I recorded a couple of quotes in my journal from some of the speakers. Among them is one from a Jewish Rabbi, who said, "The Dayton Peace Accords caused a ceasefire but not reconciliation. Peace is above and beyond human endeavor." And from a Catholic priest came, "There is only one race — the race of humanity. There's only one language, and that's the language of the heart."

---

3 Filipovic, Zlata. <u>Zlata's Diary</u>. London: Penquin Books Ltd, 1994, pp. 35-36, 42, 61.

It would be so helpful if meetings like this conference would be held in every community around
the world. People would find that we are basically
all alike with the same zeal for life and survival, the
same love and concern for family and others, and
with similar interests in many areas. And maybe, just
maybe, people might learn that nothing is solved by
picking up guns and destroying others' lives, families, and property. Will people around the world ever
learn that? I hope so!

MORE PICTURES OF AND INFORMATION ABOUT
GUATEMALA III'S MEMBERS AND EXPERIENCES CAN BE
FOUND AT:

http://sites.google.com/site/
peacecorpsguatemala3/

INDEX

Red Cross, 17, 18, 81
Reeves, Elva, 229
Rivera, Diego, 87
Ruehsen, Dr. Moyara, 252

S

Salamá, Guatemala, 149
San Antonio, Guatemala, 129
San Antonio, TX, 63
San Benito, El Petén,
    Guatemala, 128
Sanderford Morrison, Lynda,
    8, 214
Sandinistas, 248
San Juan, Chamelco,
    Guatemala, 204
San Juan Comalapa,
    Guatemala, 117, 241, 242
San Manuel Chaparrón
    Guatemala, 188
San Marcos, Guatemala, 143
San Miguel de Allende, MX,
    124, 189, 229
Santa Catarina, Guatemala,
    147
Santa Cruz County, CA
    (cycling club), 267
Santiago Tuxtla, MX, 199
San Vicente Pacaya,
    Guatemala, 141, 242,
    243, 244
Sarajevo, Bosnia, 279, 280, 281
Sayaxché, Guatemala, 70, 71,
    204, 208, 209
Schlesinger, Arthur, Jr., 27
School Construction in
    Guatemala, 131, 176
School-to-School, 69
Schwartz, Betsy. See
    Markland Schwartz, Betsy

Schwartz, Brenda, 205, 211
Schwartz, Chris, 189, 196, 203,
    205, 210, 211, 212, 213
Schwartz, Mike, 243, 248, 275
Schwartz, Nikki, 205, 211
Segregation (racial) in US, 14,
    47
Selma, AL, 219
Shell Oil Company, 149
Siebert, Dave, 37, 108, 275
Sklar, Joe, 85
Smith, Ashley, 142, 148, 204, 205
Smits, Dave, 25, 45, 50, 51, 52,
    54, 55, 56, 108, 166, 233
Smits, Patricia (Pat) Garity, XV,
    31, 34, 45, 50, 53, 56, 109-
    117, 119-124, 166-168,
    170, 233, 235-39, 242
Smits, Susana María (Susie),
    34, 110, 111, 117, 121,
    122, 233, 242
Snyder, Dave, 7, 141, 242
Snyder, Sally, 7, 141, 242, 243,
    244
Solis, Javier, 87
Sololá, Guatemala, 241, 243
Soviet Union, 13, 28, 29, 214
Spanish (learning the
    language), 9, 45, 81, 83,
    89, 93, 112, 129, 148, 165,
    234
Special Forces (aka "Green
    Berets"), 32
Stapleton McAvey, Susan, 22,
    184, 185
Station Elena, Guatemala, 70

T

Tabasco, MX, 199, 201
Taber, Doug, 108

15260813R00164

Made in the USA
Charleston, SC
25 October 2012